FENG
SHUI

FENG SHUI
The Way to Harmony

Albert Low

Pelanduk
Publications

Published by
Pelanduk Publications (M) Sdn. Bhd.,
(Co. No: 113307-W)
12 Jalan SS13/3E, Subang Jaya Industrial Estate,
47500 Subang Jaya, Selangor Darul Ehsan,
Malaysia.

Address all correspondence to:
Pelanduk Publications (M) Sdn. Bhd.,
P.O. Box 8265, 46785 Kelana Jaya,
Selangor Darul Ehsan, Malaysia.
e-mail: *pelpub@tm.net.my*

1st printing 1993
2nd printing 1994
3rd printing 1995
4th printing 1996
5th printing 1997
6th printing 1998

Perpustakaan Negara Malaysia   Cataloguing-in-Publication Data

Low, Albert
   Feng shui: the way to harmony/Albert Low
   ISBN 967-978-448-7
   1. Feng shui. 2. Divination. I. Title.
   133.333

Printed by
Laser Press Sdn. Bhd.

To all my clients who have in one way or
another contributed to the realization of this book;
through them, I have gained
invaluable experience.

Contents

A late Ching representation of a geomancer consulting his magnetic compass to select a city site.

Foreword

For more than 3,500 years, the Chinese practised the art of Geomancy as part of their culture. This ancient art of living in harmony is a branch off from the Tao philosophy; it dictates that Man and his Universe must be balanced in one form or another to avoid unnecessary calamities. Commonly known as Feng Shui, "Feng" carries the meaning the Breath of Life or Wind, while "Shui", on the other hand, is generally known as Water, a prime life-sustaining element.

In the practise, the stress on *chi* as an invisible force is said to be present in all animate and inanimate objects. For the mere instant such as the configuration of landscape, mountains, serpentine rivers and shapes of land whether they are good or ill are said to bear their own distinct symbols and meanings.

It was only during the Sung Dynasty (AD1126-1278) that Wang Chi and others formulated and systemized *feng shui,* which settled it into two schools of thought; the Fukien School which emphasizes the relationship of the planets and the Kiangsi School which relates the importance of landscape of *chi.*

For the Lo-pan or Compass which was invented for marine purposes, these so-called magnetic wonders were later implemented in *feng shui* work by practitioners.

Presently Feng Shui is still widely practised and is favourably accepted by many. But as the practise itself sometimes run into the realm of the unknown, it gives rise to the notion that Feng Shui itself is but a subject of a pseudo-science.

Whatever it is, whether through the arrangement of furniture, location of entrances or having a fountain here or there to strike a proper balance with *yin* and *yang*, there are sometimes answers to them that sound logical.

There are also times that proper answers to certain questions we seek now is not available to our questioning mind. Thus to disbelieve is of course, not disprove, and to believe is not to prove. But in truth if through practising the Art of *Feng Shui* would evoke mysterious forces in our favour to enhance our well-being, it is all that matters most.

Albert Low Yoong Shin

Acknowledgement

This book would not have been possible without the support of several individuals who have played an important part in its conception. There are especially several persons who have to be mentioned and thanked for their contribution. People like P.C. Shivadas, who is now the Group General Manager for the New Straits Times Press, who first coaxed me into contributing articles on *feng shui* to the paper. I would also like to express my appreciation to the Managing Director of Star Publications, Steven Tan, who was instrumental in getting a column on *feng shui* started in *The Star*. Behind the scenes, Davin Arul, *The Star's* Editor of "Section 2", helped me to edit the articles to suit the taste of the public.

There are also many people whom I have not met, but who have had a hand in the publication of my work. All I can say is a sincere "thank you" for their contribution. Last but not least, I would like to thank members of the public who have supported the *feng shui* column; on my part, I hope they have benefited from the information presented.

This book is based on research and personal experience on the subject for more than two decades. I had earlier thought of presenting this work in a more technical form but after much thought and consideration, I decided to present it as it is. Reading it will not make you a *feng shui* master, but I hope the knowledge gained here may somehow enlighten you. If I have failed to present it well, then I must say that it is human error on my part; for the principles of *feng shui* have always been constant.

1 *Visions of the Mind*

To the ancients, dreams were visions from the gods trying to convey messages to them while they were fast asleep. The invisible ones would silently stroll through a room and implant messages and thoughts in the dreamer's mind.

It was a privilege to dream because it was believed that only a few "chosen ones" among the masses were in tune with the celestial beings and could channel their sacred messages to the rest. They were sometimes called foolish dreamers for their minds lived in another time or dimension.

But sometimes, a few of them were revered.

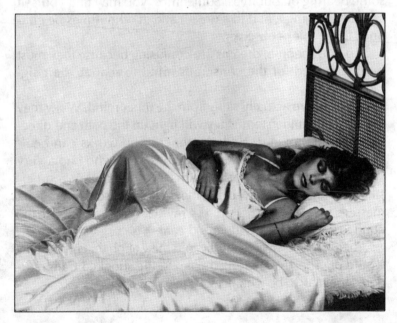

Today, science tells a very different story. To dream while we are fast asleep is very normal. Dreams normally occur during the REM or rapid eye movement phase of sleep. Dream research has found that everyone dreams while asleep. Some of us may recall dreams as shadowy, vague events while other rare individuals may be able to describe their dreams in spectacular fashion, recalling the tiniest of details.

And there are some who swear they have not dreamed for a long time. It is not that they are lying; it may be simply because, in the early years of their life, they considered dreams unimportant events and often set them aside. Because of this, dream patterns to such people would become faded and obscure until they would not be able to recall any dream at all – even though they still have them.

Carl Gustav Juṅg, the Swiss psychologist, believed that dreams hold the key to man's unconscious mind. He believed that the inner mind of man is the spiritual mind that is infallible. Through dreams, we can foretell coming events that may have some bearing on our lives. Sometimes, you may find yourself actually playing a part in a dream and at other times be confined to the role of observer.

To most people, dreams are confusing because they must be interpreted for the conscious mind to realize their significance.

Dreams are actually signs from the inner mind. Whey they are correctly understood, they will light up the path and direction for the dreamer. How the inner mind works can be illustrated by the story of an Arabian Caliph who had a very strange dream. In his dream, all his teeth fell out. As a superstitious man who believed that the dream had some important message in relation to his future, a mystic was summoned to the court to interpret the mysterious dream.

Rather tactlessly, the mystic told the Caliph that his parents would die shortly. Hearing the news, the shocked Caliph ordered the man to be whipped.

Another mystic was then summoned to the court to interpret the strange riddle of the dream. As an experienced man, wise in the use of words, he told the Caliph that he would outlive his parents and reign over his kingdom for many years to come. The overjoyed Caliph, upon hearing the good news, rewarded the man handsomely before sending him off.

Here is a situation where a dream came to the mind in a symbolic form. As Jung believed, inner visions from dreams play an important part in our lives when properly interpreted.

2 *The Interplay of Forces*

The Chinese, in practising *feng shui* for more than 3,000 years, are convinced that the environment and its latent forces affect our lives and well-being.

Most of us fail to understand that living in an environment which is out of harmony can create havoc in our lives. The saying "To have a house facing a tiger's mouth" means certain death. This could be a symbolic saying used when a *feng shui* master sees a rock or mountain having a concave shape that resembles a tiger opening its mouth.

Again to the Chinese, saying "surely die" does not necessarily mean physical death – it is only a saying. For a businessperson, it could mean failure in his or her business while for a politician, it could mean the end of his or her political aspirations.

The situation is exactly the opposite of a dream. Dreams arise from the inner mind, while this is a case of the environment affecting a person's life through his unconscious mind.

The way of studying shapes and forms from the environment is the oldest *feng shui* system and is known as the Form System.

The discovery and usage of the compass was later implemented in the reading of *feng shui* and is known as the Compass System. Compared to the Form System, the Compass System is relatively new.

One may ask how the forms of an environment can have such drastic effects on our lives. We can only speculate on theories that are thought-provoking rather than explained by supernatural beliefs.

When a Zen Master says that everything is "Maya", we think he is nuts. The word "Maya" comes from the Sanskrit word meaning "illusion". Actually, the Zen Master is speaking on a very deep level of consciousness. He sees a space and calls it an illusion because nothing animate or inanimate exists in that particular region. When he sees a solid table he also states that it is an illusion. It sounds silly and absurd because we know that the solid table is there. But as a man speaking of a "higher place", he simply means that the object is real and yet not real because he speaks in terms of energy levels.

It is atoms vibrating at a certain low rate that form the table. So when the Zen Master speaks in terms of high energy levels, ironically everything is but an illusion.

Walking physically through walls is quite an impossible task to perform. But there are stories from ancient times, and whispers of monks and holy men adept at performing these superhuman tasks. Speaking in the context of physics, it is not possible. But what if the human body can change the rate of its vibration to a higher, finely-tuned level? Walking through walls and concrete would then be child's play.

We say that in *feng shui*, the principle theory of certain occurrences can be traced to shapes of objects and their environment because all these forces are working at a higher plane of existence or dimension.

To stress again the earlier example of the house facing a "tiger's mouth", imagine that the house is merely a sizzling, vibrating collection of atoms and the so-called "tiger's mouth" is one as well.

Since every solid object is but a mass of vibrating energy or atoms, then each object can give off positive or negative forces. These actions normally take place on a higher plane of existence to affect people's lives. When men fail to recognize this interplay of forces, they become victims of their own ignorance.

3 *Not the Place to Call Home*

There are some locations considered unsuitable for homes. Such locations can have adverse effects on the people living in them, leading to poor health, loss of money, etc. In some cases, such bad luck can be averted by the use of an eight-sided trigram or *Pakua* mirror.

1. **T-Junctions**
   This is not a good site because spirits, travelling in a straight line, tend to inhabit such a building. The building, too, takes the brunt of a negative whiplash created when motor vehicles turn at junctions.

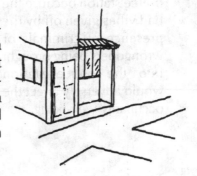

2. **Trees in Front**
   If there are trees blocking the main entrance to the house, this is symbolic of joss-sticks on the altar and in the same way, the occupants become the "sacrificial lamb".

7

3. Hill in Front

A high mound or hill in front of the house represents obstacles for the occupants. The occupants will not prosper in business. The hill will also obstruct or block the flow of *chi* into the house.

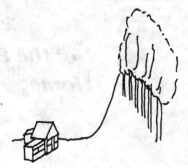

4. Police Station

It is considered bad luck to live in a house facing a police station because the bad vibes given off by the presence of criminals or wrongdoers being brought into the police station would adversely affect the occupants' well-being.

5. Temple

Similarly, a house facing a temple is not good because spirits can be found hanging around temples. Furthermore, people go to the temple to pray most often when they are down and out. The bad vibes they give off will affect the occupants of the house.

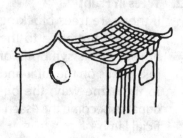

6. **Prison or Hospital**
   Similarly, houses facing prisons or hospitals are bad for the occupants.

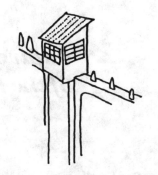

7. **Cemetery**
   A house facing a cemetery is not favourable for its occupants.

4 *Unfavourable Fronting of the House*

1. Bad Smell
A giant rubbish bin in front of a house gives off bad *chi* or smell thus bringing bad luck to the occupants.

2. An Axe Problem
Having a bus-stop in front of a house is like having to face the front of an axe as the shape of the bus-stop sign has the likeness of an axe.

3. Sign of Mourning
An electrical pole with the middle part painted white symbolizes an arm band for mourning. The occupants will not be happy staying here as the sign of sadness is always found in front of the house.

10

4. Tree in Front

A tree in front of a house also blocks off the flow of *chi* if the house faces a good direction.

5 *Facing Ruin*

Subway Station

A house facing a subway station – or an MRT station, as in Singapore – is not a very good choice for a home. *Chi* travels downward into the subway station, thereby siphoning off the wealth of the owner.

Factory with Tall Chimneys

Having a factory with tall chimneys or smokestacks in front of a house is considered bad *feng shui* for the occupants. The chimneys represent joss-sticks being burned, symbolizing a sacrifice for one who has been a victim of unfortunate circumstances.

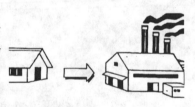

Fence with Many Square Holes

A house facing a fence with many square holes is also considered bad *feng shui*. It symbolizes a net which enfolds the house, trapping the occupants and inhibiting their progress.

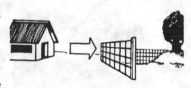

Car Park

A car park in front of a house is not very favourable for anyone who is ambitious in his career. The parking area simply means that everything becomes stagnant for the occupant. There will be no progress for those who stay there.

Army Camp

A house that faces an army camp or base is also considered bad *feng shui* for most people, because very few can tolerate the *yang chi* or aggressive lifeforce emanating from it. An army camp is often full of tension as soldiers go through dif-

ficult training to make themselves battle-ready, and because of this *yang chi* emanating from the camp, the surrounding areas are not conducive to a peaceful life.

Old Fort

One may find that the occupants of a house that faces an old fort or historical castle may likely encounter earthbound ghosts or spirits. During ancient times, places like these often had torture chambers or dungeons where unfortunate peo-

ple suffered and died. As a result, their unhappy spirits often wander around these areas, even though the site of their deaths may have long since fallen into ruin.

A Long Tunnel

A house located near a long
tunnel is considered bad *feng
shui* because when a strong
wind blows through the tunnel,
it creates an eerie sound that
may affect the occupants in one
way or another.

6 *Don't Stay Under the Cable-Cars*

1. Bad for Health

Having a cable-car system running directly over your house is bad *feng shui* in terms of health. As the electrical cables above produce an energy field, the human body's own "aura" is disrupted, affecting those who live in the house over a long period of time.

2. Luck Reduced

A house that faces a flyover brings bad *feng shui* because the force produced by the constant flow of traffic and *chi* dissipates the house's "luck". It is also a bad place to live because of the noxious gases emitted by the continuous stream of passing vehicles.

FORCES OF MASS TRAFFIC

15

3. Stepped On
The people living in a house under a pedestrian bridge are believed to get "stepped on" all the time by people crossing overhead. There will not be much progress for those who live in such a house. Furthermore, irresponsible people may throw things down – and it is a bad sign to be constantly showered with other people's garbage!

4. Negative Turn
A simple child's slide in a playground may seem rather harmless but to a *feng shui* expert, it indicates a negative turn of fortunes when the slide slopes down towards a house across.

5. Unhappy Feelings
Living too near a casino is also considered not favourable for good *feng shui* because of the negative, unhappy feelings that radiate from the gambling den – the result of too many people losing money there.

16

7 Stumbling Block to Good Luck

Water Hydrant

A water hydrant in front of a house does not necessarily mean that the owner will receive an abundance of money as symbolized by water. Since it obstructs the main entrance, we can say that it brings about the opposite instead.

Side Pillar

The side pillar of a neighbour's gate also acts as an obstacle to good *feng shui* for the house facing it.

Roman-Style Pillar

A bungalow with a Roman-style pillar directly facing its own entrance may also be a bad choice in terms of *feng shui* as it blocks good luck flowing into the house.

17

Swing

A house facing a playground with a swing directly in front of it symbolizes a guillotine slicing or cutting the owner's wealth in half. It will not be a good place for a person involved in business to live.

Huge Billboard

A huge billboard in front of a house also blocks good fortune coming in.

Multi-Storey Building

A house that faces a multi-storey building will receive a double dose of bad luck. First, the building blocks the house's entrance and second, it casts a long shadow over the house.

Two Highrise Buildings

When a house faces two highrise buildings across the road, with a narrow alley between them which directly faces the house, it is considered to be very bad *feng shui*. It is believed that energy from the sky will travel through the narrow gap between the two buildings and strike the house across the street. In *feng shui* it is known as "Thunder striking from the Heavens".

18

8 *Tell-Tale Signs to Watch Out For*

A wrongly-positioned clothes-line, seemingly harmless telephone pole cables, and even a hidden drain can impede the flow of *sui* (water or luck) into the premises. Watch out for these tell-tale signs if you wish to be lucky.

Disharmony
Sharp Razor Edge: A house having a sharp razor edge pointing towards its direction is also bad *feng shui*. Such a shape, also known as "secret arrows", shoots its fiery rays of *chi* causing disharmony to those who live in the target area. To be on the safe side, it is best to move to a new house.

Money shiphoned off
Hidden Drain: An outlet draining water, located directly opposite the main entrance of a house, is considered as having bad *feng shui*. As water or *sui* flows away from the house, the occupants will have their money gradually siphoned off.

Double Bad Luck
Sliding Fortune: A house with its main entrance blocked by a support cable for a telephone or electrical pole angled at 45 degrees is in for double dose of bad luck. First, the cable blocks luck and second, its sloping position represents luck sliding downwards for the occupants.

No Progress
Clothes-Lines:
Stringing clothes-lines directly in front of the main entrance of a house acts as a "stranglehold" on the occupants. Residents of such a house will not progress far in life or professionally. The only remedy is to reposition the clothes-lines away from the entrance.

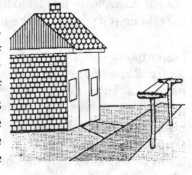

Unseen Danger
Underground Stream or River:
A house built on such a land may have its luck carried away by the current. The unseen danger is often not discovered until it is too late.

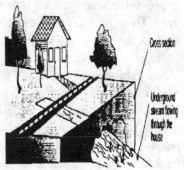

Cross section

Underground stream flowing through the house

9 *Check Direction of the Stream*

Where you build your house can affect your physical and financial well-being as well as that of your family.

1. **Flight Path**
   Housing estates situated near airports are generally considered unfavourable. This is due to the negative *chi* created when planes are flying too low to the ground. This is harmful to those who are not mentally and physically strong.

2. **Straight Stream**
   A stream or river that flows straight past a house is considered unfavourable because it sweeps away with it all the wealth that could have been the occupants'. But it does not mean that a river near the house is unlucky. One must observe the direction in which the water flows.

3. Railroad Tracks

A house facing a railroad track is considered unfavourable as each time a train passes by, its vibrations shake the very foundation of the house. This is symbolic of instability in health, wealth and family affairs.

4. High-Tension Wires

People living near high-tension wires will be affected by the strong energy emitted. This energy can affect a person's aura field, causing mental disturbance. When the Europeans first erected telephone wires in China, the Chinese tore them down, realizing that the magneto-electric power will disturb the harmony of the human body.

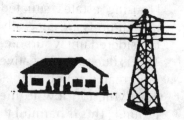

5. Transmission Stations

Research and studies conducted has shown that staying near power stations, transmission stations and TV and radio stations is hazardous to health as the radio waves emitted are so strong they can cause disharmony within the human body.

6. North-East

In *feng shui*, the north-east is also known as the Devil's Door. One should not have homes or doors facing this direction as occupants will suffer from ill-health.

7. South-West

Likewise, the south-west is considered the Devil's back door. It is unfavourable to have a home facing this direction either.

10 *On the Receiving End of a Roof*

The shapes of some buildings not only portend disaster for the occupants but also for those who live next door.

1. **Split-Level Roads**
   Some roads are split-level in that houses on one side of the road is at a lower level than those on the other side. This is un-favourable, especially for those on the higher level, if the roof of the lower car porch is aligned such that it cuts the main entrance into half. This causes a disrup-

tion to the flow of *chi* or energy force, resulting in illness to the occupants.

2. **Knife-Shaped Roofs**
   The knife-shaped slant of the roof of this high-rise building acts like a "guil-lotine" that "cuts" the low-rise house in two. This will result in trouble for the oc-cupants of the house.

24

3. Dead-End Roads

A house situated at the end of a dead-end road is considered unfavourable because homes at the beginning of the road would have absorbed most of the *chi,* thus leaving very little for the last house.

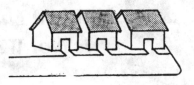

4. Higher Field

If a house faces an open field that is slightly higher than it, the field obstructs the flow of *chi* to the house. Therefore, it is not favourable.

25

11 *When Lady Luck is Not Wanted*

1. Crab Symbol

This is recommended for casinos. The two wings of the building look like the open claws of a crab, waiting to catch its victims in its clasp, thus making the odds in favour of the casino. The presence of the lake is of importance as the water or *sui* of the lake represents money for the casino. There is also a one-way road up and down. Gamblers are welcomed the front way, but everyone leaves by the back way.

2. Birdcage

The birdcage-shaped casino places the odds against the gamblers as they, like the birds, are caught in the cage and thus part with their money. However, gamblers stand a better chance if they were to enter by the back entrance via the hotel proper.

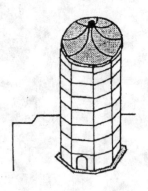

26

12 *More Feng Shui for Homes*

1. Open Waste

It is bad *feng shui* to have a home near a sewage pond. As bad *chi* from the waste rises, even trees planted here to hide or block it have very little effect.

2. Fiery Perimeter

It is unhealthy and not conducive to harmony to have the perimeter of a house built in this "fire" shape. If you live in such a place, the family would have many quarrels and misunderstandings because fire generates much heat.

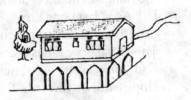

It is also considered bad *feng shui* to build or live in a house facing a place where people are lonely and (or) suffering. Negative *chi* is being created and gets into the ether or atmosphere. It may easily affect the occupants of a nearby house.

3. Tomb Perimeter

This house has its perimeter built in a Spanish style but to the Chinese mind, this design looks like a tombstone. It is bad *feng shui* to have these tomb-like structures surrounding your house as the living and the dead must be far apart. These shapes may mislead and attract spirits which would make this their resting place.

4. Double Trouble

These two bungalows have their fronts facing each other at a T-junction, creating double trouble for the occupants of both houses. The worse off of the two is the bungalow on top of the hill. As a "last bungalow", it is difficult for *chi* to reach. This bungalow faces more bad luck as its entrance slopes down towards the driveway. In *feng shui*, it means money is rolling away, thus making it dificult for the tenants to accumulate or save money.

13 *Added Risk at a T-Junction*

1. Danger can befall a house and its occupants facing a T-junction when the road is too steep.

2. Since a house at a T-junction faces a direct stretch of road, it is always easier for a robber to observe the house before planning to rob it.

3. The headlights of vehicles can disturb a sleeping occupant at night, therefore causing restlessness.

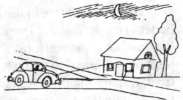

4. Houses located at T-junctions are frequent "highways" for ghosts and spirits as they always travel in a straight line and penetrate solid objects like houses.

29

If you try to talk about T-junctions to a housing developer, he may just shrug his shoulders and try to avoid the issue.

For almost 3,000 years, the belief or superstition that a simple T-junction can bode ill for the occupants has been embedded in the minds of the Chinese. It can be said that for this long period, they have all been foolish, or become wiser by acknowledging that those who went against this belief often fell victim to their own "ignorance".

Nowadays, housebuyers are more mindful of location when deciding to buy a house. After all, buying a house is neither a simple matter nor a small investment.

Those more shrewd and calculative than most might take buying and selling houses as a short-term business investment. When times are good, they would sell the house for a profit.

But how easy is it to sell a house which is situated at a T-junction? Or can he even sell it at all, despite repeated advertisements in the papers?

Some buyers who consider themselves "immune" or who do not consider the T-junction belief, may take the opportunity to knock down the price with the developer, who may be willing to part with it for a low price rather than leave the house vacant and without a buyer.

What truth is there in the belief that a house at a T-junction bodes ill for the owner? There may be several answers, depending on what angle you look at it from. For instance, take a house built on a T-junction at the foot of a steep, downward-sloping road. If speeding vehicles fail to stop in time or if their brakes fail, they may cause damage to the house or even injury to the occupants.

A T-junction house also leaves a clear stretch of road from which a would-be robber can have an unobstructed view of the place. He may take a slow walk or just drive several times along the road, just to observe his intended target before making plans for a break-in.

Light can be beneficial to man when he is its master. But light can also be a nuisance when it shines directly on our faces or into our rooms when we are asleep. Such is the situation in having a bedroom facing a T-junction. The occupants may have a hard time getting to sleep, with the frequent "display" of lights on his bedroom wall.

Lastly, the Chinese believe that all spirits and ghosts travel in a straight line. They believe that when a house is located at the end of a T-junction, the occupants will have a lot of unwelcomed invisible visitors passing through the house. And if the occupants' life-force or *chi* is not strong enough, they will eventually fall ill.

14 *Warding Off Bad Chi*

So much has been described about the devastating effect of a T-junction and how it can affect the household. But there are certain temporary measures that can be taken to balance the energies at work and bring them into harmony.

ACTION 1   The Mystical Way
The *Pakua* symbol is placed over the doorway of the household to deflect whatever bad influences and forces coming towards the house.

ACTION 2   The Natural Way
Change the fencing of the main gate and door from the junction by using natural, that is, growing thick hedges to absorb the impact of the bad *chi* coming from that direction.

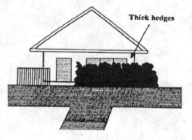

Thick hedges

ACTION 3 The Natural Way II

The power of a huge tree planted here absorbs the impact of the bad *chi* coming from the T-junction.

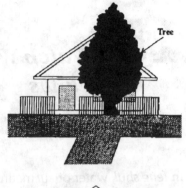

ACTION 4 The Artificial Way

Change the fencing of the main gate and the door from the junction and put up a brick wall. The front of the wall must be painted white. Of all the cardinal colours, white is the one that best reflects heat and energy.

ACTION 5 Surrender

Giving in to the forces of the T-junction by moving to a new home is a wise choice – if one can afford it, of course!

33

15 *Watch Where the Water Flows*

In *feng shui,* water or *sui* means money. If one is not careful of how the water flows from his home or office, his wealth may quietly flow away without him noticing it.

House that always has no money
This owner has built a high wall around his house probably to give his family more privacy and protection from outsiders. The wall has lots of weeping holes to drain off water should it rain, otherwise pressure from trapped water in the ground may crack the wall. But having the front wall with too many holes means that money is flowing away before it can enter the house, making it hard for the owner to earn and save money.

Car Park atop Office
To have an office below a car park is also bad. In a car park, nothing is stable. As vehicles move in and out of parking

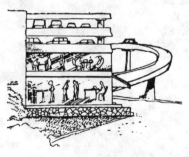

bays, this results in uneven and unbalanced weight of the *chi*. Siting a business here is bad.

Hilltop Condominium and Drainage System

A condominium built on top of a hill will give the tenant a superb view of the city. But the developers made a mistake by building huge water drainage system which runs straight from the building to the bottom of the hill. Because of this, they will be set by financial difficulties before the building can be completed.

Office Building with Portholes

To have an office building with portholed windows is bad *feng shui* if it is too near the sea. The sea, with its huge mass of water, will attract all the wealth of the building through the holes.

16 *Lower Ground Woes*

When comparing higher and lower grounds, *feng shui* masters always suggest that the lower ground has bad *chi* and many disadvantages. There are sound reasons to prove that this is so.

In the ancient days, having a house, town, village or castle on low ground would mean that the occupants would be at a disadvantage when invaders attack from a higher ground. The attackers would have a better vantage point and staging point for their raids.

Natural Disaster

There are also three types of natural disaster that could befall the occupants of a house on lower ground.

1. Loose boulders, stones and rocks from higher grounds could threaten those living below. Tremors and erosion could cause rocks to fall, thereby injuring the occupants or causing damage to property below.

2. After a heavy downpour, a river may burst its banks and flood low-lying areas.

3. In cold, mountainous countries, vibrations or sudden noises could trigger an avalanche, which could be disastrous for those living on the slopes or valleys below.

Modern-Day Hazards

In modern times, fumes from factories and motor vehicles would gradually find its way to the lower ground; those living in such an environment would breathe in this foul air, thereby putting their health at risk.

Another "modern risk" is living below a sharp bend or curve in the road as a careless or drunken driver might fail to negotiate the bend properly thus causing the vehicle to go over the edge. Those living below would definitely be at risk.

A hill or mountain tends to block the light from the rising sun from reaching a low-lying house. It also casts a pall or shadow on the house which brings an unnatural darkness to the building. Such a situation can cause the occupants to miss many good opportunities in life.

Finally, there is the risk of one's privacy being invaded by a busybody or peeping tom living on a higher level.

17 *Above It All*

Higher ground has numerous advantages and is preferred when picking a site to build. Occupants of buildings located on high ground are above it all – they have a panoramic view of their surroundings, are far from noise and pollution, and may even live longer.

Thrones are always on raised platforms so the sovereign can watch over his subjects and survey his kingdom. If a king has his throne on lower ground, his subjects will be above him and take the opportunity to overthrow him.

During medieval times, castles and fortresses had high ramparts and tall towers to deter invaders and intruders. It was virtually impossible for enemies to scale these high structures.

And those secured on higher ground always had the advantage of observing enemy movements and so will be better prepared to plan their defence and organize counter-attacks.

Living atop mountains or on high altitudes offers obvious advantages. Mountain air is cleaner, cooler and more refreshing than the polluted atmosphere of the lowlands and cities which are chockful with fumes from industries and motor vehicles.

With purer air, the lungs are taxed less and the body received all the oxygen it needs to stay healthy. Thus, it is no surprise that South Americans of certain tribes living in Andes live to a ripe old age. Furthermore, residents on higher ground have no worries about floods and are seldom affected by disasters and war. This leads to a less stressful existence and longer life.

Even if you can't afford a cool mountain retreat, you can take comfort if you live on high ground in the urban area. Such residents have the advantage of being able to observe what goes on below.

Such foresight may cause some to postpone their appointments and meetings or to take a different route when they spot traffic jams or accidents.

18 *"Fired" Upon by Bad Luck*

Cross at Entrance
A cross formation caused by staircases across the entrance of a building acts as a barrier to the flow of *chi* into the building.

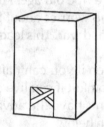

Cannons
An old cannon pointing directly at a building "fires" destruction at that building although it may serve as nothing more than mere aesthetic purposes for the building in front of which it is sited.

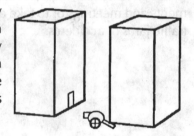

Flyover Obstruction
A building sited next to a flyover is considered not good for businesses especially at the point directly obstructed by the bridge. The constant flow of traffic is symbolic of frequent changes in the company's fortunes – in other words, there is no stability.

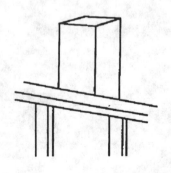

40

Triangular Building

This is not favourable as the shape of the building is not balanced.

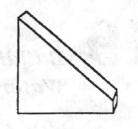

Valley Location

A building that is located down in a valley or where the road is higher is bad *feng shui*. This is because *chi* and light find it difficult to get into the building. Dust and dirt will also fall onto the premises caused by pollution.

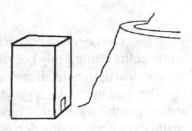

The Dwarf

The particular building in the centre is shaped like a rocket and at the time it was built, was probably good *feng shui* as it would mean its tenants would go far in politics and business. But within a few years of it being built, this "rocket" building was surrounded by many high-rises that had far more stories than it.

This has changed its *feng shui* somehow. The *chi* or energy force is oppressed and the "rocker" is now like a dwarf among giants.

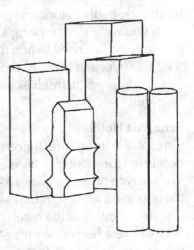

41

19 *Buildings at the Waterfront*

Feng shui can be much poorer if we do not take a good look at some of the Hong Kong buildings that are built according to geometrical designs in alignment with *yin* and *yang*.

The reason to take a good look at Hong Kong is that the majority of the people are Chinese. Their forefathers came from mainland China and the rich businessmen at that time brought along their *feng shui* men – a "transfer of technology" during those old, harsh days when the mind of an intellectual was respected.

Today, the success of Hong Kong's citizens is partly due to hard work, partly to luck and partly to *feng shui*.

If you were to visit Hong Kong on a tour, you would most probably be surprised to find the tour operator babbling about *feng shui* here and there. And during lunch-break, the bosses of large companies themselves will take their turn to boast of their *feng shui*.

Peninsula Hotel

One of the most prestigious hotels in Hong Kong, where a Rolls Royce picks up guests at the airport on request. A bird's-eye view shows that the hotel is shaped like a horse-shoe magnet facing the sea. From the aspect of *feng shui,* it draws and captures water or money with its outstretched arms.

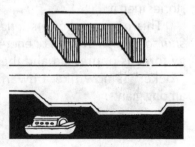

Edinburgh Place

This is a typical example of a building in Hong Kong shaped in the form of the wood element facing the ocean. A wood-like symbol of a tree fed with water signifies perpetual growth. Many buildings in Hong Kong are shaped like this.

Ocean Centre

This is a shopping complex which has a wood-based shape attached to a U-shaped magnet facing the open sea. The shape of this shopping complex came about from the belief that it would attract luck and money.

Harbour City

This complex of shops, hotels, offices and luxury apartments links up with Ocean Centre and Ocean Terminal. From a bird's-eye view, the Harbour City main complex is square in shape, forming the wood element. As it is near the harbour, the base of its buildings are shaped like anchors, to keep a strong hold on business.

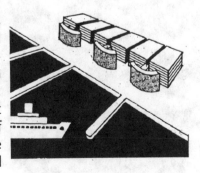

New World Hotel

It is not enough to site your building near water. The surrounding area should be carefully studied to see if there are any obstacles that may block *feng shui*. A good example is the New World Hotel, built in the shape of an arrow. The reason is that the Cross Harbour Tunnel linked to Hong Kong island is like a rope that may strangle the business, and the only way to make sure that all is well is to create an arrow-shape to cut through it.

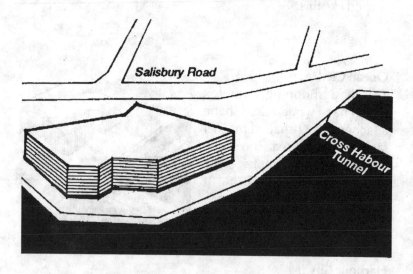

20 *Finding the Right Spot*

The study of *feng shui* does not confine itself to shapes, terrain, homes and large buildings. This intricate art goes beyond these and even touches on islands and whole countries.

Feng shui on such a large scale is not often heard of because many geomancers are either not knowledgeable enough or the task is too big for them. So, they often leave it until they feel they have reached a higher level of knowledge or experience to handle it.

It takes only the very best and elite *feng shui* master with years of toil and experience to deal with this subject because of the delicate nature of the job – finding out exactly where on the land that the power of the *yang* or life *chi* lies. Once the geomancer has identified these sites where the good *chi* lies, his work becomes easier. He is immediately able to scale down his work before going into the finer details.

You can compare this sort of work to the hi-tech super spy satellites in orbit. Suspended in the dark, silent void of space, they serve as an invisible eye for the wealthy nations that can afford them. When the satellite is in the right position, over the country or site to be observed, its mechanical eye will take in all the details of what is happening there. If a smaller or tighter focus is required, computers are able to enhance the satellite's findings.

Feng shui is similar in the sense that it can be focused on a specific area before the intricate analysis is performed by the geomancer.

When a geomancer makes a general comment that a particular shopping complex has good *feng shui* without elaborating, you will see many people scrambling for a lot there. As soon as a particular lot becomes vacant, the stakes in securing that place become increasingly higher.

It is not unusual, however, to find that 20 to 30 per cent of the businesses operating in a place with good *feng shui* may actually be on the edge of financial difficulties, despite the crowds that flock to the complex. The reason is that when a geomancer says a place has good *feng shui,* he is only making a general comment on the entire building. But when shoplots face "down" escalators, are located near toilets or facing long passageways (like the notorious T-junction), things are different.

All buildings that have good *feng shui* would also have areas that have weak spots that should be avoided. If someone says that a building has 100 per cent good *feng shui,* it might either be a joke or a serious statement from an amateur, or even a conman.

21 *A Place to Stand Firm*

Archimedes (287-212BC), the Greek genius and mathematician, said: "Give me a place to stand firm and I will move the world." This statement has held true until today.

To talk about having a good place to stand is like having your feet firmly rooted to the ground.

In Chinese arts of self-defence, new students are initially taught to stand for long, gruelling hours in the horse stance. The horse stance is a semi-squatting position, and students may have to assume this pose for half an hour daily at first, more as they progress.

For beginners, it is very taxing and not an easy task to perform. At the start, they may feel their legs wobbling like a cyclist after a tyre punctures. After a short while, weary legs may be laced with wild fire which runs madly up the spine before racking the body with pain.

But the master knows what he is doing for his students. A good solid foundation must be laid before other lessons are taught.

To achieve the highest levels, nothing comes easy; there are many dropouts in martial arts schools where this is stressed, and not surprisingly.

Only the fittest and the best become good enough to stay on and remain faithful to their master. Dropouts, on the other hand, cannot point accusing fingers at the teacher for they failed because they could not pay the price. The price involves self-discipline, hours of dedicated practice, a genuine effort to achieve perfection and even mind over matter.

Parents know that their baby must crawl before he can walk. Such early movements help strengthen tendons and bones to set the stage for the child's future development. In a short while, the child can then walk upright. In the beginning, the child may lurch about clumsily or fall down. With time and encouragement from the parents, the child will eventually be able to stride confidently unaided. This gives the little fellow independence; he can happily walk or dash from room to room in the house, or play hide-and-seek with his parents. We say that when a child has reached this stage, he has finally found his own footing.

Though you may share the same time and date of birth with others, it is the place of birth which determines your future. Each animal sign under the Chinese zodiac is allocated its own position and also a point in a "golden" triangle.

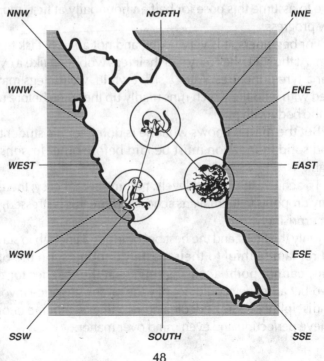

A Chinese physiognomist or fortune-teller shares a common view in predicting the fate of a person who walks with his feet not fully touching the ground. This person will not receive the full benefit of the *chi* from the Earth, thereby shortening his lifespan.

A *taichi* master would know the secret of the Earth *chi* or *yin chi*. Every delicate movement of his is finely co-ordinated with his breathing. He taps the *yang chi* or heavenly *chi* from the air, and when his feet are firmly planted on the ground, taps the *yin chi* as well. This fuses the two forces of *yin* and *yang*, and the balance struck between them benefits the *taichi* master's health.

In ancient China, there was once a rumour going around that the country had two Emperors; if not, then it had two beggars instead. This gossip somehow reached the Emperor's ear, and he immediately called a meeting of his ministers and advisers.

The Emperor demanded to know the story behind these rumours. All the royal advisers stood tight-lipped eyeing one another. The impatient Emperor looked like a volcano about to erupt. Then one of the royal advisers told the Emperor the story. Instead of being angry, however, the ruler was amused. He then commanded his advisers to solve this mystery. It turned out that a commoner had been found to share the same time, date and year of birth as the Emperor.

According to belief, an Emperor and commoner born at the same "celestial time" should result in there being two Emperors, or two beggars. However, there was only one Emperor.

The search for the solution to this mystery was begun. After months, no answer was in sight. As a last resort, the search was opened to the public, along with the stern warning that anyone giving a foolish or false answer would be beheaded.

At first, it seemed that no one would dare take the challenge, with so much at risk. One day, however, a wise man arrived at the palace with the claim that he could solve the

49

mystery. He was then brought before the Emperor, who had been intrigued by this mystery for so long.

Calmly and respectfully, he told the ruler that he was indeed the only Emperor. Although the time and date of birth was shared, the place was not – and he concluded that the place of birth also determined the destiny of one's life. Therefore, he said, the reason one child had become Emperor and the other had not was because of their respective places of birth.

To determine your rightful place to stand, you must first find out in which direction you are in harmony. The "signposts" for this lies in the Chinese horoscope.

The twelve animals of the Chinese zodiac are in harmony in groups of three, or "golden triangles" as shown on the map of Malaysia on the previous page). Each animal also has a particular "facing" and a good direction for someone born under that animal would be this direction, along with those of the other two in its golden triangle. The four golden triangles and directions for the animals are given below:

1. Rat – North, Dragon – East South-East, Monkey – West South-West;
2. Ox – North North-West, Snake – South South-East, Rooster – West;
3. Tiger – East North-East, Horse – South, Dog – West North-West; and
4. Rabbit – East, Sheep – South South-West, Pig – North North-West.

In order to find your "heavenly direction" you should look at the corresponding group. If a person is born in the year of the Rat, his true direction is North. Because the Rat gets along fine with the Dragon and Monkey, their own directions will also be in harmony.

22 *A Building's Face is its Fortune*

The shape of mountains, rivers and landscapes is a natural work of art. It takes the genius of wind and water to erode the land into shapes that fall in harmony with the forces of Heaven and Earth.

To the ancient Chinese, this was the work of the mighty gods who would cut, mould and chisel gigantic rocks into mountains, valleys and the like. Their work was looked upon and admired by mortals who thought that these unseen powers came and went at their whim and fancy, shaping things whenever they felt like it. They had no fixed timetable, as time was considered irrelevant to these eternal beings.

When rain comes from the heavens, its first physical contact is with the high mountains. The mountain is like a rendez-

Pyramid skylight

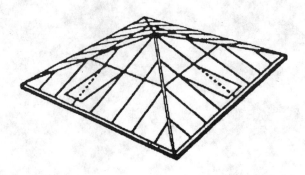

vous for the powerful forces of wind and water, a focal point where the two are destined to work together – to sculpt, smoothen and shape its faces and surroundings.

Perceptive *feng shui* masters recognized these powerful mountains for what they were, and so advised clients not to confront them when building their homes. This was done so that the full force of the bad luck emanating would not fall upon them.

Modern man, with his sophisticated machines, can easily conquer the land and change its face to suit his needs or desires. Natural landscapes can be cleared or flattened in a much shorter time than they took nature to build, merely to make way for highrise buildings. These newcomers would then be built in different designs and shapes conjured up by the imaginations of their builders, regardless of whether they are in harmony with their surroundings.

23 *With an Eye on Harmony*

What do you do when you realize that a building you own is not shaped to be in harmony with the natural forces? It would be quite impossible, unthinkable even, for you to blow it up and start all over again.

A costly mistake like this could not be easily undone; whether the problem can be rectified and the building eventually "fine-tuned" to be in harmony with nature depends on the ability of the *feng shui* expert called in to help.

Sometimes, certain work involving large buildings can become too difficult for a geomancer to handle in the *feng shui* sense.

The client's choice of geomancer is thus very important, and if he chooses unwisely then let him beware.

An experienced *feng shui* master, when working on a multi-level building or house, always takes great care to look at the exterior or facade of the building before proceeding with his work.

Actually, a building's exterior is a primary factor in helping the geomancer make his final decision as to whether the building is properly aligned with the *yin* and *yang*.

In physiognomy, an expert can easily analyse a person's character from his appearance. So it is that in *feng shui,* an expert can tell from a building's exterior if it will bring good or bad luck to the occupants.

One of the worst shapes to have on multi-level buildings or houses is that of a triangle, which is known as the "fire shape". If a building has already been constructed in such a shape, improvements can only be made to a certain extent. It requires a special kind of "plastic surgery" to change this building's face to enhance its fortune.

24 *Built for Success*

Buildings come in all shapes and sizes and have various significance in Chinese geomancy. We will now feature some examples of highrise office and commercial blocks, and a stadium, which incorporate elements of strength, success, integrity, harmony and even aggressiveness in their exterior designs.

The General's Attire
The renowned Chiang Kai Shek Memorial in Taipei is a mammoth building, with its stylized twin-tiered Mandarin roof, a symbol of the general's struggle. The roof typifies the hat worn by generals of the imperial court many centuries ago, a monument befitting a person of General Chiang's stature.

Building with Foresight
The Hongkong Bank building is one of the most expensive in the colony. It has a unique modern, classic look. At a glance, the facade shows up as spiders spinning webs, which is somewhat akin

to someone who is forever busy making money.

The top of the structure is even more interesting. The protrusion resembles the head of a man. From a certain angle, it looks like the man is peering into a pair of telescopes – searching the horizon for a better future. Certainly a building with foresight.

Wave of Success

One uniquely shaped building is the Hua Ting Sheraton Hotel in Shanghai. From afar, it very much resembles a series of huge waves, one atop the other. Since water or *sui* in Chinese symbolizes money, the layers of waves are like stacks of currency. Thus, the building will encounter success upon success.

The Firm Fists

The imposing twin towers of Hong Kong Financial Square look like clenched fists which represent firmness, solidness, strength and integrity. These qualities will surely exude a sense of confidence among the business community in the colony.

25 *Safe and Solid Buildings*

Harmony of Heaven

From the air, the Olympic Stadium in Seoul, where the 1988 Games were held, is a picture of harmony. It resembles an ancient Chinese coin (round on the outside and with a square hole in the middle) which represents heaven and earth. The stadium's shape gives it a sense of balance; perfect for the venue where athletes from nations throughout the world gather in brotherhood and friendly competition.

Another classic example of the harmony between the forces of earth and heaven is evident in a square of rectangle-shaped building with a circular structure on its rooftop.

The Rocket

The side of this building is designed in the shape of a rocket, wide at the base and tapered at the top. It is a good place for those who are ambitious and seek lofty positions in life. The rocket aims at reaching the top fast and nothing is beyond its reach. Those who occupy such a building, especially politicians, will be so driven.

Coffin-Shaped Windows

Windows shaped like coffins adorn this building which should make a perfect office for an insurance company, especially in life insurance, because the spectre of death as represented by the morbid shapes will discourage early death of clients. In that case, the insurer will not have to pay out large sums in claims.

Steps to Heaven

This large building is one solid block with well-balanced stairway-like structures on both sides. The glass facade reflects the wide blue yonder of the sky, as if "grasping" the heavens. Symbolically, it means whichever way one looks at it and whatever the goals, aims and aspirations will be attained.

26 *Feng Shui and Rubbish*

The word "rubbish", classified in *feng shui* and linguistic terms, means unwanted or unused goods. Objects such as a pile of old newspapers, empty bottles and boxes are some examples of these items.

Strictly speaking, most of us are not professional collectors who hold on to things in the hope that they may someday become collectors' items or antiques. On the contrary, most of us simply postpone the dumping of such things, constantly telling ourselves that we will do it the next day. But because of the human weakness of procrastination, tomorrow often never comes, in most cases.

Feng shui masters do not only look at the shape of houses and buildings, or their location and facing, to determine if a place has "luck". They also have a sharp eye for details like placement of furniture, pictures and other objects in the house. When certain objects are really out of place, the geomancer will point out this fault. It may cause some embarrassment to the owner and his family if they are sensitive to such remarks.

There are times when families, feeling guilty about not tidying up the bedrooms or some other part of the house, may cook up stories to cover up their untidiness.

Sometimes, there may be a funny situation when a husband brings home a *feng shui* man to the horror of the unsuspecting wife. The wife may need to excuse herself and rush into the bedroom to clean things up as much as possible before emerging, red-faced, to welcome the geomancer into her home.

Remember that geomancers are not health inspectors look-ing for health hazards. Nor are they fault-finders poking fun at people and laughing at their expense.

Remember that to be hygienic means to live a healthy life. You will also find that a clean environment more pleasant than an untidy one.

When the geomancer points out things that are not in order, he is only trying to correct the mistakes his clients have made, in the hope that they would put things right.

Unfortunately, old habits die hard.

A huge pile of old newspapers is easily noticed, whether it is in plain view (on top of or under tables) or hidden under the stairs. In fact, because of the secluded location, one home-owner actually filled up the space under his staircase with six months' worth of old newspapers! A geomancer whose ser-vices he engaged pointed out that too much bad *chi* had been stored up in that spot thanks to the old newspapers.

The owner immediately began removing the newspapers when, to his horror, a large black rat darted out from under the pile, followed by several cockroaches. The houseowner stood frozen on the spot, clutching his pile of old newspapers with a look of confusion and shock on his face. It is a fact that when an area is unhygienic, it attracts many lower forms of life which find it a cosy place to live. Cockroaches feed and breed there, lizards prey on them and a small area to humans becomes like a miniature war zone, where a vicious game of hunter and hunted is played out between sheets of newspaper.

This small world will continue to thrive day after day, as long as it is undisturbed by humans. If it continues to go unnoticed, it will quietly continue to siphon off *chi,* or lifeforce, which is used up by these smaller creatures.

After all, rubbish will attract more rubbish.

27 *When Emptiness is Not Really Empty*

An Empty House

As emphasized in the previous chapter, emptiness is not really empty. A house vacated by its owners for a long period of time

is not a good sign. Houses are bought for many reasons: to live in, or simply as an investment for the future. A person who owns too many houses may have a slight problem because he cannot live in all of them at the same time. The best solution is to rent them out, even at a low rate, so they can all be occupied at all times.

It is commonly held in the practice of *feng shui* that when houses are occupied, the very breath that each occupant takes creates a kind of warmth in the surroundings. At the same time, it gives the house "life". The reverse effect can be seen when a house is left vacant for a period of time. An empty house is like an empty shell, providing a roof for an odd wandering spirit or two that may stop over. It may be a problem getting rid of these unwelcome visitors when new human occupants move in.

It is believed that setting off firecrackers in the house may frighten these visitors out, making room for the living. One top executive, who is a bachelor, lived alone in a huge rented house. Every weekend, he would invite his colleagues over for a party.

You can just imagine a house like that, in a prime location, being quiet and peaceful from Monday to Friday. Then, come the weekend, it would go crazy with blaring music and revellers having a party until the early hours of the morning.

The host, of course, was pleased as he believed that it was infinitely more preferable having people make a lot of noise in the house, rather than some nocturnal visitors.

A space is never really empty when we see nothing there. Life giving substances like oxygen are most likely present, along with other gases like nitrogen, hydrogen or carbon dioxide.

So even though we may see nothing occupying a space, we cannot always say nothing exists there (unless it is a vacuum).

It is common to find people who like to keep empty shoe boxes, or any kind of box for that matter. When asked why they have this habit, they are often lost for words. One person even said that he kept empty boxes to pack his things in case he decided to move house. When asked by his geomancer when he was moving, he just shrugged his shoulders. Why would he hire a geomancer if he intended to move?

Anyway, open space does not have a negative aspect. It is when emptiness is enclosed that it has a bearing on our lives. Trapping air in boxes for a long time creates stale or dead *chi*. Many of us would know the feeling upon entering a vacant house that has been locked up for some time. The closed windows and doors trap the air which becomes stagnant and foul. It is only when the windows and doors are opened, to let in new air in exchange for the old, stale air, that we can feel the freshness.

So do not store too many boxes unnecessarily in your house. Otherwise, they may snap up and entrap the life-giving forces in the building, depriving those living there of their share. As we need the vital breath of *chi* to remain in harmony with nature, then this life-giving force should not be kept from us.

28 *The Hidden Power of Colours*

Once, in the United States, a thief broke into a house and stole a television set. The very next day, to the astonishment of the victims, the stolen set was found on their lawn. Attached to it was a note which read: "No colour, no fun!"

This may sound funny, but it is no joke to the millions of us who have made it a daily habit, almost a ritual, to glue our eyes to the television set. Imagine what it would be like if some act of physics suddenly rendered all the images transmitted in black and white!

Man does not appreciate or recognize the value of things until he loses them. It is true when we talk of colour, too – we only appreciate it once it is gone.

Colour plays a very important role in the lives of professional artists, fashion designers and interior decorators, many of whom could probably not function without it. The ancient Egyptian priests, renowned for their arcane arts, and the Chinese *feng shui* masters share a common belief – that colours have powerful "vibrations" of their own. They knew the secrets of how to unleash and harness this power and use it to their advantage.

There isn't much difference to that of an ambitious general negotiating matters of state with his rivals, or a politician making a call to the people in his election speech to convince them to vote for him. Both these men may have their own little secrets, wearing selected colours to bolster their chances of success. Their choice of colour may work on the people's subconscious to influence them towards seeing things their way. Every day, our subconscious is assailed by the forces of colour as chosen by such shrewd individuals.

A group of psychologists, intrigued by this controversial topic, did a study on a particular red bridge that had a history of people committing suicide by jumping off it. Why the red bridge, and not bridges of other colours nearby?

The moment of truth finally came after the psychologists obtained permission from the town council to have the bridge painted another colour – the "neutral" colour of white.

The following year, to their astonishment, the bridge some-how failed to attract any would-be suicides – changing the colour of the bridge had something to do with it.

The incident described earlier can be compared to the case of a client who, when consulting a geomancer, complained that the old folks living in his house always seemed to fight daily.

The geomancer found that the walls and doors inside the house were all painted red and without haste, recommended that his client paint them a more "cooling" colour. Shortly after this, the "war" within his house came to an end.

Stories like these are hard to believe but are actually com-mon cases handled by geomancers. One of New York City's top modern-dance teachers discovered that when he put grey costumes on his dancers, they became apathetic and lethargic. But once he changed the colour to warm red, the dancers be-came livelier and showed much individual expression.

In the United States, doctors are also becoming increasingly aware of the value of colour in patient recuperation. One sur-geon went to the extreme of decorating the rooms in his clinic in different colours. One room was decorated completely in blue, from the walls to the rug, curtains, bedspread, lamp-shades, towels and paintings. The other three rooms were done up in lavender, yellow and green.

The blue room was used for cardiac patients; lavender for those recovering from heart surgery or with respiratory illnesses; yellow, an active colour, for renewing energies and influencing the circulation and digestive systems; and green, primarily for calming nervous patients.

The surgeon discovered that the lighter the shade, the more relaxed the atmosphere within the room. As each colour has many shades, the decorator must know the right shade – just as a cook knows how much salt and seasoning to add to his food to get the right taste.

The New York Times also ran an article which said the effect of colours in classroom on children was a matter of concern to education officials. When architects got together with educators and psychologists in Baltimore, Maryland to discuss the new school buildings, they decided that there should be proper lighting and old blackboards ought to be replaced with green ones. The cafeteria would serve the students food on plastic trays in various colours. The classroom walls were painted in wedgewood blue and trimmed with bright yellow.

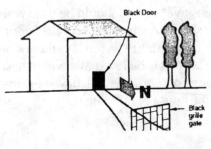

Black Door

Black grille gate

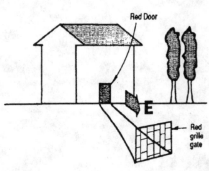

Red Door

Red grille gate

Sensitive colours. Black should not be used on gates, doors and walls which face north or south, while red should not be used on those facing east or west. It is believed that when these two colours are wrongly placed, they have negative effects on the occupants.

One superintendent of schools reported that vandalism had greatly diminished and he firmly believed that the entire tone of a community can be raised by the children's awareness of the beauty and cheerfulness of certain colours.

Many primitive races used colour dynamics in their cultures. Some colours were used in rain dances, others at times of celebration, and some even in times of war. Modern warfare has not changed that much in terms of camouflage. Whether in primitive times or today, there is no doubt that Man knows how to manipulate colours to his advantage.

In *feng shui,* colours are neither good nor evil but possess a neutral force. As one man's meat is another man's poison, such is also the case with colours. People should understand the characteristics of the different colours before trying to fit them into their environments.

In *feng shui,* two main colours – black and red – stand out from the rest as the most "sensitive" and so should be used with caution. For instance, black should not be used on gates, doors and walls which face north or south. Just as red should not be used on those facing east or west. It is believed that when these two colours are wrongly placed or used, they will have negative effects on the occupants of the house or building.

29 Colours and their Meanings

Did you know that those who wear brown are often plodders; people who are nervous or highly-strung should not wear red; or that violet is the colour of the martyr? The following are the main characteristics and true meanings of various colours.

White

A novice martial arts exponent starts off having a white belt to signify his ignorance and innocence. A bride wears white to show her purity.

White is known for its brightness and as a "clean" colour. It is a neutral colour which, when shined into a prism, emerges as all the other colours. It takes no sides in the affairs of men. In metal and precious stones, it represents silver and diamond.

Yellow

A dash of red and orange from the colour yellow. This colour has the power of the rising or morning Sun and was a favourite colour among Sun worshipers. Usage of yellow is believed to allow the cultivation of intuition, ambition and helps in the acquisition of wisdom. Yellow represents gold.

Orange

This colour symbolizes an inclination towards social activities. Those who use this colour often will seek the security of group activities and will often be found working for other people.

The colour of the Sun as it finally retreats below the horizon each day also represents a lack of confidence in men to do things independently unless they are led. This group of people are said to "follow the crowd".

Red

A fiery, passionate and highly emotional colour, it is the colour of intense heat, divine love and blood. Like a dancing flame which goes out of control, spreading in many directions and wreaking havoc.

Red is beneficial to those who are lackadaisical and need more "life" in their system. For those who are hyperactive and sensitive, red should be used less for it is known to arouse the nerves easily, resulting in dire consequences. The precious stone associated with red is ruby.

Black

The colour of the earth, darkness, wickedness, negation and death. It is the colour of magic and is a favourite of the stage magician whose profession is to fool and deceive an audience through trickery or sleight of hand, often with the aid of black backdrops and equipment.

It is also the colour of night and the unknown. To some who understand its meaning, it can simply represent a new beginning – life after death.

Brown

A firm colour. The person who surrounds himself with this colour seldom rises to any great heights in life. He prefers to go plodding along, making a steady living.

Grey

From the mixing of black and white, grey is created. It is the colour of uncertainty, fear and falsehood. It is also a deceptive colour.

People who prefer grey appear to be conformists although they usually bid their time until their own interests can be served – usually at the expense of others.

71

Green

This is the colour of tranquility. It is also the colour of money, as in the United States dollar. It has a soothing, restful influence, preserving the eyesight and calming nerves. Those who give green prominence in their dressing like international travel.

A side-effect of this colour when overused is to cause a person to become envious and greedy. That is why people who are jealous are said to be under the influence of the "green-eyed monster". The precious stone associated with green is Emerald.

Blue

Blue is the colour of the sky. It represents spiritualism, thoughtfulness, consideration and care. Blue expresses faith, truth, constancy and fidelity. The precious stone associated with blue is Sapphire.

Violet

This colour belongs to the hermit who dwells in mystery. The philosopher, the poet, the dreamer, the writer and the visionary all like this colour. Violet often signifies love and truth, or passion and suffering. Therefore, it is a colour often used by martyrs. The precious stone associated with violet is Amethyst.

30 *Believing in Luck Transfer*

Can luck be transferred from one object to another? Scientifically, it sounds absurd and illogical. It is indeed a difficult subject to grasp and while there is some truth to it, it is often stranger than fiction.

An unusual story was related by a businessman who met an acupuncturist living in a remote village. The businessman fell ill and his relatives took him to see the old gentleman, who was reputed for his vast knowledge of the human body.

While making his diagnosis, the acupuncturist asked a few questions, only to be answered curtly by the man's relatives, who seemed to be in a hurry to go somewhere else.

After studying the case, the acupuncturist finally began his treatment by sticking needles into the patient's body with great care in order to create a balance of forces within the man. The acupuncturist turned out to be a good conversationist, engaging the patient in chatter to distract him from the many needles poking his body.

The patient, meanwhile, answered his questions like a dreamer in a hazy, semi-conscious state. The acupuncturist was in complete control of the conversation. Near the end of the treatment, he declared that because of an act by the patient's father long ago, his family was now suffering a spell of bad luck.

The patient was surprised because his father had actually done what the acupuncturist described – and in so doing, sealed the fate of his descendants.

The patient's father, who owned a fleet of lorries, had once ordered his workers to remove a boulder from an abandoned quarry which was facing his home. The man ordered that the rock be placed beside a large pillar at the main entrance to his house. By doing so, he hoped to force lorry-drivers to slow down when they enter the compound of his house. In that way, he thought, there would be no danger of a careless or impatient driver damaging his house.

Not long after this seemingly trivial deed, the old entrepreneur passed away peacefully in his sleep. However, the cause of his death, whether old age or illness, could not be determined.

The responsibility of running the business fell to his sons but, somehow, things got out of hand. Business foundered and the company's debts escalated.

An emergency meeting was called to look for a solution to its many problems but eventually, the majority decided to throw in the towel and wind up the company.

The abandoned quarry across the road, which had closed when the company running it went bankrupt, was reopened when another firm took over its operations.

Surprisingly, after a short time, business picked up and buyers for their rocks seemed to appear out of nowhere. The new owner of the now-booming business became a millionaire.

The old man should have left the quarry alone. By moving the rock to the front of his own house, he brought a surge of negative energy from that vicinity into his own home. And in turn, the removal of the rock brought about good fortune to the new quarry owner.

There are many rags-to-riches stories where the poor man who makes good refuses to discard or part with certain items which he had been using for a long time or which had been of some use to him during his lean periods.

There are often stories of self-made millionaires who hold on to their old cars jealously although they now own expensive

new cars because these cars were at one time their only means
of transport. Of course, it could very well be for sentimental
reasons. Then again, many of them believe that the old
"junkheap" may have brought them good luck and success and
will not part with them at any price – for it would mean giving
away their luck.

31 *The Transfer of Emotions*

A man was once asked by a good friend to accompany him to a relative's funeral. This man had no blood ties whatsoever with his friend, but agreed to attend. Almost everyone was sobbing or wailing mournfully, having lost someone dear, while some others tried to hold back their tears.

After about three hours of sitting around comforting his friend and watching the mourners cry their eyes out, the man decided to call it a day and return home.

While he was driving home, he suddenly felt sad. It was strange; after all, he had no blood ties with the deceased.

In this kind of incident, you could say that by consoling his good friend in a time of sorrow, he had relieved his friend part of that sorrow, which had then become "attached" to him.

In this instance, we can truly say a transfer of emotion had taken place. We sometimes get the kind of inert feeling when someone "passes the buck" to us without our knowledge.

One must therefore be truly careful whom he meets, or the kind of companions he mixes with. Otherwise, a positive-thinking character may end up becoming negative over time because of this intangible influence from others.

A social worker may face this problem; by helping society, he may meet lots of negative people who come to him to find a solution to their many problems. Provided he knows how to detach himself from the problems he is trying to solve, he may often feel tired after each session.

The amount of negative people in contact with him would take some of his positive aspect away, draining his *yang chi.*

It is safe to say that a depressed person who goes to a lively party may return home uplifted in spirit. And that a jolly character who meets a group of negative-thinking people may find himself struggling to get by if he allows them to engulf and dominate his thoughts and feelings.

Stroking a small needle with a magnet several times will make it temporarily magnetic. As the magnet is the stronger force of the two, it will imbue part of its power into the needle. Similarly, this can happen when dominant forces or attitudes encounter weaker ones.

32 *The Cooker*

A man who had just rented a house moved in after paying the usual deposit. For the first few months, life in the house seemed ordinary – until the man realized that members of his family had taken ill one after another. He consulted his personal physician who enjoyed a "roaring trade" as the man's relatives marched into his consultation room one after the other.

At the end of the session, each of them was given medication and sent home. For the next couple of days, everyone took his medicine, but there was no appreciable improvement at all.

Returning to the doctor, they received a second prescription of the same medicine.

Another week of pill-popping went by. And again there was no result.

In desperation, they called in a *feng shui* consultant.

The geomancer came to the house at the appointed time and day, where he found the family gathered outside, anxiously waiting for the man they hoped would be able to reveal the source of their mysterious illness. With his intricate compass, the geomancer first studied the surroundings, jotting a note here and a note there before deciding to enter the house.

Inside, he checked out the main hall, dining hall, bedrooms and kitchen before tracing himself back to the family members who had stood patiently in the compound waiting to see what he had to say to them. To their utter disappointment, the geomancer told them there was nothing wrong with the house, as far as *feng shui* was concerned.

Dismayed, the family – who had expected the man to pinpoint some negative aspect of the house somewhere, and therefore identify their problem – paid the geomancer his fee.

Just before he left, the geomancer turned around and asked the head of the house if he or any members of his family had taken anything left behind by the previous tenant.

For a short time, everyone was silent, trying to recollect. Then a family elder spoke up, and assured the others that he had seen a brand-new ceramic cooker in the kitchen, while they were negotiating with the owner before renting the house. After moving in, he said, he made good use of the "free" cooker to prepare some meals. This new information made the geomancer decide to stay back while he considered its meaning.

Finally, he concluded that misfortune had befallen the family as a result of using the cooker. He said it was left behind by the previous tenant with the sole purpose of leaving his bad luck behind. The cooker represents food and bounty, and it is believed that whoever "inherited" this mysterious gift would exchange their good fortune for the bad fortune left with it.

Of course, to point an accusing finger at an innocent-looking cooker sounds silly but there may be more to it, as we will find while delving deeper into this strange subject of *feng shui*.

33 *The Five-Clawed Dragon*

History shows that the Chinese have a fondness for *objets d'art*. Exquisite paintings, immortal motifs in ceramics, fine silk, translucent jade, lacquer, bronze and furniture speak of this fondness from the distant past to this very day. Their grand designs, worked by master craftsmen, cannot be measured by today's products produced on a commercial scale through mechanical means.

Nothing was left to chance during those days in creating a fine piece of art. For example, a carved stone dragon could have taken a master's lifetime with the patience to carve it out of a rough stone into a masterpiece. A wrong strike of the chisel and years of hard work would be wasted, as the piece would have to be junked and the job started all over again on a new stone. If fortune smiled upon him, the fate decrees that his work turns out to be a masterpiece, even then he would have to suffer

the casual glances of the uninitiated. But those who have an eye
for such fine works see things differently.

Every fine curve left by the master has its own secret meaning. Life can be added to the dragon by the look in its blazing
eyes, and its power can be measured by how tightly the dragon
clenches it claws. Sometimes, you wonder how the stone
dragon gets all these positive forces. Perhaps it was the master
craftsman who, somehow, by virtue of being immersed in his
work, left all his *chi* or lifeforce into the dragon, thus imbuing
the object with the "breath of life" itself. Those who see it will
be full of admiration and awe, as if the mythical dragon is real,
merely frozen in stone.

In fact, Chinese art and design are permeated by a connect-
ing sense of the wholeness of things. Its extensive vocabulary of
design motifs is based on timeless principles – spirit, rhythm,
life and movement. True Chinese design is never meaningless
ornamentation. Its exquisite beauty of animals, plants and objects often have a hidden meaning which puzzles the casual
observer. For example, a dragon is not just a dragon. You have
to count the number of claws it has. In the olden days of the
Chinese monarchy, ordinary folks could only use dragon motifs
with three or four claws.

If a person accidentally used a five-clawed dragon motif in
his attire, he would be roughly dragged out by the imperial
guard, whipped and have his head lopped off. The "Son of
Heaven", the Emperor, was the only one with the right to use
the motif.

You may wonder why.

During the time of ancient Persia or Iran which was then a
powerful warrior-state, wars between neighbouring states and
other rivals were common. When the Persian army was victorious, thousands of prisoners of the defeated army were made
slaves.

One interesting thing to note is that, in addition to the
prisoners being tied to one another and being dragged into

slavery, they also had their thumbs covered or bandaged with cloth. This is to symbolize their complete submission to the victors.

In the study of palmistry, the possessor of a straight, strong thumb has a strong will and cannot be easily manipulated by others. A thumb that is too flexible and bends backward easily indicates that the person has a weak will and his thoughts can be easily influenced by others: He will find it difficult even to make decisions for himself.

Psychologists have also observed that a person who always clenches this thumb within all four fingers is, by nature, an introvert. Such people are normally very shy and believe that others are superior to them. Indeed, the thumb is so powerful that at times you may hear a comment that a husband is under his wife's thumb.

As palmistry itself denotes that the thumb represents willpower, then it may be one reason why the five-clawed dragon is considered supreme. Thus, it was reserved only for use by the Emperor, who was divinely chosen to rule the Dragon Throne.

The divinely-chosen Emperor must use the five-clawed dragon to show absolute power and the heavenly mandate to rule his kingdom.

Today, even after the last Emperor of China, Pu Yi, has lost the mandate of Heaven to rule and the imperial system abolished in place of the communist system, you may not be safe using the five-clawed dragon in your designs unless your blood is of the royal blue. Who knows – by using a five-clawed dragon motif and design you may somehow, at the right time and right place, conjure up the power of the dragon and doom yourself to disaster.

The Chinese have a saying: "Never wear a hat that doesn't fit you."

34 *Motifs with a Motive*

In ancient China, everything had a purpose. Even putting up a painting or some designs on the wall of a house would always have some hidden or inner meaning.

The richer the owner, the finer and more exquisite his *objets d'art* would be as he could call upon the finest artists and craftsmen to do his bidding.

If an artist could produce a masterpiece, then he would be paid even more than the original fee.

The fine work of art would then be put up in a place of pride where the owner and his peers could admire it over a cup of tea.

Why do some people go all out to get such fine works of art, when every stroke of the artist's brush is a blow to his wallet?

There are many reasons why people do this, apart from an artwork's commercial and aesthetic value. For example, a person who puts up a painting of a flying eagle, soaring high in the sky with its powerful wings outstretched, may have done it to show his interest in martial arts or the military. The strong, warlike eagle may also show his deep desire and ambition to rise to greater heights in his profession.

Abstract and modern art coming from many styles in today's paintings have compounded the situation. Many people choose to buy paintings without knowing their hidden meanings. They believe that if there is an empty wall in their house or office, it is best to fill it up with paintings, and all will be well.

But in *feng shui,* on the contrary, a person who decorates his home or office in this manner may actually be carrying out a destructive act, especially if the wrong picture is put up. For instance, if a businessman hangs up a cold winter scene which depicts leafless trees and not activity, he is only courting trouble by choosing such a "negative" scene. He may wonder why so many of his business deals fail to go through. The winter scene in his office may have something to do with it. And if he happens to change the scene to a more positive one, perhaps his business will improve.

Ancient Chinese motifs and paintings are still very much in use by modern-day Chinese to decorate their homes and offices because the symbols are easily understood.

Crane
A large wading bird with long legs and neck. This graceful bird symbolizes longevity and purity. Magistrates and judges in ancient China usually had this motif in their chambers, where they would deliver their judgment. Therefore, this bird also signifies justice.

Butterfly
The butterfly represents the return of the soul of someone close who has just passed away. It also symbolizes the spirit of joy and happiness.

Phoenix

It is doubtful that anyone, even the ancients, ever saw a real phoenix. This bird which can burn and rise from its own ashes symbolizes self-sacrifice and rebirth. The action is repeated again and again until perfection is attained. The phoenix is also said to bring peace and harmony.

Lotus

The lotus signifies purity. This is also because the lotus is often found growing in muddy ponds amidst unpleasant surroundings, and yet is uncontaminated by its environment. It also represents creative power.

Goldfish

For a businessman, a live goldfish is a very powerful sign to have in the house or office, because it enhances the luck and future of the occupant. Take care of the number you rear, however, or it may have negative consequences. When consulting a geomancer, this is one question you may wish to ask.

Bat

This nocturnal creature is seldom used because not many people know its true significance, simply because they fear it. Others, however, believe it to be a very intelligent creature that sees things from a different perspective because it hangs upside-down when at rest. Some bat motifs are also found in places of worship because the bat is also known for its philosophical outlook in the spiritual world.

Water

Water, in Cantonese, is *sui* which also means money. As the most important "element" for sustaining life after air, it can take the shape of its surroundings (such as a container) with ease because of its fluidity. Lao Tzu, the founder of Taoism, used water as a symbol in his teachings.

Like blood running in the human body, it must be kept continuously moving or the body will die. The same goes for the commercial world, where money is deemed as important as blood. When its circulation is interrupted, then financial "death" follows. Many businessmen like to have paintings of water hanging in their offices, where the flowing water symbolizes money flowing in.

Clouds

The symbol of clouds represents heaven. It also implies that "the sky's the limit" and there is always room for improvement or promotion. It is a positive sign and spurs the belief that one can soar in life to as high as one's thoughts permit.

Peach

The peach is known as the "fruit of the immortal". Some Chinese immortals can be seen in works of art carrying this fruit as a sign of longevity.

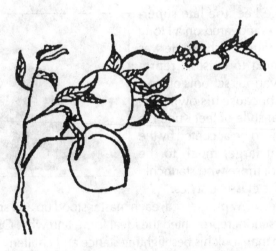

35 *Head of the Matter*

An ancient Chinese proverb says: "Cut the head and the body will fall." This statement from the wise men of the past still has bearing on the present because of the simple truth it represents.

The Chinese have made the head the most important part of the body; it is treated with utmost respect and should not even be made fun of or hit in jest.

Bruce Lee, the late superstar, once appeared on a Hong Kong evening TV show. He was seated next to masters representing various schools of martial arts because his own controversial style of Jeet Kune Do had come to be accepted by the public at large, much to the chagrin of those who staunchly held to the classical styles.

As the show progressed, each master stood up and spoke on how his school represented the ideal form, and why. One middle-aged man took his best fighting stance and challenged each of the panelists to push him over. One by one they got up, but failed.

Finally, it was Bruce's turn and the man taunted him in Cantonese: "Come on, young punk, let's see you try."

Bruce wasted no time. He stood up, walked slowly to the man and with lightning speed, laid him low with a hard punch to his face.

"Why did you do that?" the others asked him.

"Because I don't push," he replied. "I punch."

This infamous act may have cost him some friends, and his standing in the colony's martial arts community, but his move was simply common sense.

Most martial artists would know that their best blows to a certain part of the body would have no effect on a man who knows how to bring his *chi* to that area. The only way to uproot a man in the above case was to knock out the "control box", the head, causing the entire body to fall.

Another good example comes from an episode of *Get Smart,* in which Maxwell Smart or Agent 86 was trapped by some enemies in a department store at night. Cornered and desperate, he decided to aim at the overhead lights and knock them out, hoping to get away under the cover of darkness. Alas, luck and his aim were not with him that day, for he missed some lights and ran out of bullets before he could get them all. Finally, as the bad guys closed in, he turned in desperation and saw the main fusebox, right behind him all along! So he managed to turn off the lights in the entire store, and got away.

Recounting this incident may seem silly and irrelevant, but who knows, there may be some other "smarties" out there who would do something like this without realizing that the main fusebox, or master control, or the head as it were, is the thing to go for.

Checkmate the king and the chess game ends. Capture the commander of an army, and his troops will lose their sense of direction. Assassinate the head of a nation and chaos will reign. If the captain of a ship is drunk when it sets sail, the vessel is probably doomed. Have lots of apprentice chefs preparing a meal without the chief cook around, and the food will probably be "off".

This is not to say that all leaders are indispensable, and in fact anyone is dispensable. But replacing someone who is in charge after he has been removed suddenly is not easy. Adjustments have to be made, the new head has to adapt, and so on.

This analogy stresses the importance of the head.

In *feng shui,* the bed is treated with importance and should not be placed in a position where a gap of one or two inches is left between it and a wall. Some "super-clean" clients say they left the gap there so they can reach between the bed and wall with their brooms to sweep away the dust that gathers there. Well, how much dust could gather there if there wasn't a gap to begin with? In fact, the headboard of the bed should be placed firmly against the wall.

You can imagine that the head has a mountain as its support, representing the strength to be acquired while one is in repose. Leaving a gap represents instability, and to sweep in the gap between the headboard and the wall will bring bad luck to the person who occupies that bed.

36 *The Magic of Mirrors*

In the story of *Snow White and the Seven Dwarfs,* a wicked witch, believing herself to be the most beautiful woman in the realm, is seen asking a magic mirror who is the fairest one of all – the answer as we all know is obvious, as long as Snow White still lives, she will never be the one.

In the early years after its discovery, the mirror held fascination for many. Early Man could only look at himself on the surface of a pond, river or stream. To see a reflected face at the time was considered seeing an illusion.

In later years, polished metal was sometimes used to reflect images, but it was found that nothing could match the mirror.

A Pakua Mirror: Reflects evil forces.

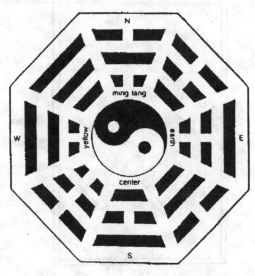

When the Europeans expanded their empires and dealt with a great many native tribes, they believed that these indigenous people had hoarded a lot of gold, silver and other treasures. To persuade them to part with their treasures the Europeans offered the natives mirrors. The unknowing natives must have received the greatest shock of their lives when their own images stared back at them from these strange objects.

Many of them threw the mirrors away in panic.

They believed that having their images reflected in these mirrors meant their souls had somehow been captured and confined within. The white men must have some kind of powerful magic, they thought. It was unfortunate that because of this misunderstanding, many of the traders were killed for stealing the natives' souls.

Ancient warriors also often had broken glass and small mirrors embedded in their armour or shields. Horses that would move in front of advancing armies also had mirrors in their headgear and armour.

The Yin Mirror: Attracts light and chi.

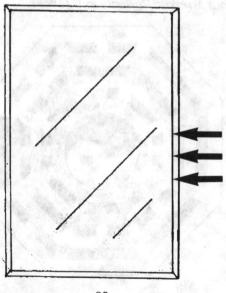

The people then believed that part of the Sun's energy could be captured with these mirrors, and transferred to the wearer, enhancing his strength and giving him invulnerability in battle. To a certain extent, the sight of a horde of bloodthirsty warriors rushing to engage the enemy while sunlight glinted in strange patterns off the mirrors in their armour must have been an awesome spectacle and could indeed have demoralized many enemies.

Stage magicians are also fond of using mirrors to help in their escape acts and creation of illusions. Special mirrors are made that reflect "false images" to mislead the audience. As one man remarked at a recent magic show, "We pay to be fooled."

Mirrors and glass have many uses. For the myopic, defective eyesight can be corrected using special lenses. For scientists and astronomers, giant telescopes fitted with powerful lenses become their eyes in outer space.

Compressed glass is used by security-conscious public figures in their car windshields and house windows – this so-called "bullet-proof glass" protects them from would-be killers.

Today, highrise buildings often have glass all round their facade for a "new look". Behind the scenes, many *feng shui* masters would have advised their clients – the builders or owners – on these matters.

Glass of different shapes and colours is known to reflect or attract certain forms of energy, causing disaster for the owner if the wrong type of glass is used that does not fit his building. The enormous sheets of glass used in today's highrise buildings might cause the sceptics to speculate that many *feng shui* masters must either be in league with glass manufacturers, or at least have invested substantially in their companies.

If not, glass manufacturers and suppliers should be grateful to them for creating a profitable market for them.

To *feng shui* masters, mirrors and glass are powerful instruments that are sometimes used to counter or balance certain forces.

When a long passage in a building is too dark because of bad planning, it gives an eerie, ghostly feeling. Mirrors can be placed at certain strategic locations to attract a flow of light and *chi* into the area, thus brightening things up and creating a sense of balance in the atmosphere.

A very rich man who, on a whim, decided to consult his geomancer before moving into his new house, was told that the house is in balance with the forces of nature, except where the garage was situated.

He advised that a *pakua* mirror be hung on top of the garage to deflect the harmful *chi* that would threaten the occupants of the house. The pakua must be specially charged with energy, which the *feng shui* master promised to supply. True to his words, he gave the *pakua* to his client the very next day.

The rich man's business improved and success came his way.

A few months of good luck passed, and one day a storm caused the *pakua* to be ripped from its place and thrown to the ground.

The next day, the owner noticed the accident and managed to find the pieces of the shattered object. The man did not fix it but instead, placed an old, unused mirror where the *pakua* once was. That sealed his fate. He soon lost a great deal of money over the next few days. He panicked and summoned his geomancer to check the house again.

The first thing that the *feng shui* master noticed upon arriving at the house was the old mirror hanging over the garage. The geomancer then patiently explained to the owner the difference between a *pakua* and an ordinary mirror.

A *pakua* reflects whatever *chi* is not wanted, while a mirror will only attract it. The owner was advised to remove the mirror, which he did immediately, and a new *pakua* was especially made to replace the old one.

A *pakua,* when charged with energy, is called a *yang* mirror. As *yang* is active in motion, this mirror will act against and repel evil forces. Ordinary mirrors, *yin* mirrors, are passive and attract *chi.*

37 *The World has Lost its Balance*

Mysterious visions have been recorded throughout history, delivering urgent messages to humanity about its future.

In 1960, three young children in Garabandal, Spain, claimed to have seen a vision of a strange, beautiful woman. The apparition, they said, told them the end of the world would be near when a hole appeared in the sky.

Air Pollution: Industrial estates contribute to the depletion of the ozone layer.

The statement did not make much sense at that time. It is only recently that the relevance of this portent has become clear, in the form of holes in the Earth's ozone layer. Such holes, over each of the Poles, are mostly caused by the release of chlorofluorocarbons or CFCs into the atmosphere.

Now, the protection against ultraviolet light and cosmic rays has been lessened. Even sunbathers who once enjoyed getting a good tan now think twice before going out to "catch some rays".

Holes in the sky aside, more environmental problems have cropped up of late. The polar ice caps are melting faster, it is said; the world's forests are being depleted; pollution is spreading fast; entire species of animal life are on the brink of extinction.

The story is the same in so many parts of the world. Because of some of these occurrences, even the world's weather patterns have changed. We hear so much talk these days of "unseasonal" heatwaves and cold fronts and floods. The weatherman's job has become so tough it may be easier soon for him to throw darts at a list of weather patterns and use the results as his forecast for the day.

In short, all this shows that the world has lost its balance of *yin* and *yang;* the forces of nature are often no longer in harmony with the presence of Earth's most destructive occupant.

If Man, the master and keeper of his own realm keeps on harming the planet, it is the "lower" forms of life that will die off first – the plants and trees, followed by the animals that live in them. Then, when it is too late, Man will find himself next on the list.

The forces of air and water are the masters of change; when so many things that are harmful have been put into them, it is only natural for the elements to spread these contaminants with the changes that they bring. Therefore, pollution may never be confined by man-made boundaries, spread as it is by the very elements themselves.

In *feng shui,* it is said that to disturb the Heavens and Earth, and to throw them out of harmony with the natural order of things, is to push the living Dragon down a steep, high cliff.

But will the powerful Dragon allow itself to be pushed? If not, Man must be very careful with his next move, for the angry creature would surely unleash a terrible vengeance on the offenders.

Water Pollution: Even rivers are littered with waste dumps due to industrialization.

38 *The Mysterious Thai Syndrome*

There are many roads that lead to the top of a mountain. You may walk around the mountain many times in a circle before deciding to ascend. You may also find yourself wandering up and down along a winding path before finally making your way to the top.

Of course, there are those who have no time for these little games and so, when they decide to climb a mountain, they take the hard way – straight up. So all paths lead to the same place over different periods of time.

Recently, news of Thai nationals dying in their sleep came to the attention of the world. In Singapore alone, reports claim that in the course of seven years, 200 out of 3,000 Thai workers had died mysteriously.

This year alone, 15 more joined the body count. It is a mystery because most of the workers who were found dead were young and healthy.

Some suggested that the fatal sleep was caused by the crowded living conditions in their work camps, where up to 30 workers could be crammed into a tent.

Looking at it logically, this sounded a bit silly. Many capable manual workers flock to rich nearby countries because of the high salaries they expect to earn.

In the first place, most of them come from poor families and are forced to move out in search of greener pastures. For instance, when I was in Pontianak in eastern Indonesia, I saw the kind of conditions the people lived in. For a moment, I thought I had been transported back in time to some pristine past when electricity had not been discovered. In most areas, the only source of light at night came from a candle.

There were no pipes to carry water into their homes, but wells had been dug nearby. When the well-water ran dry, the men, women and children of the village could be seen cleaning themselves in a huge drain running outside their homes.

The level of water, maybe two or three feet, means that to take a bath, they would have to clamber down some wooden steps into the water and lower themselves into it. Of course, those staying downstream would have to take a very early or late bath because of all the dirty water flowing towards them.

Tourists who happened to walk past the road and saw naked grown-ups splashing happily about in the water were often shocked. But to the locals, this bathing in the open had been a routine since their childhood days.

In many poor countries, you can easily find people living in such conditions. A single waterpipe in such areas would have caused sudden "human traffic jams".

So in my opinion, the living conditions in the work camps, could not have adversely affected the workers' health as they had experienced such conditions back home.

If that was the cause of their demise, then why not the workers from places like Indonesia, who lived under similar conditions?

Drug
Recently, speaking to a Thai man, I heard a different version of what made the workers die. He believed there are certain employers who make their workers toil through the day and night and when I said it was not possible, he insisted that it was.

He said these people took a certain kind of homemade potion to give them the extra "oomph" to work through day and night. Nicknamed "Crazy Horse", this drug had a catch – the user would have his entire system burnt out from using it, and death would be imminent.

It reminds me of a marathon runner who, out of the blue, signed up for a run at the last minute. Without conditioning your body to run, tackling this distance can be a hazardous undertaking. There have been cases of people collapsing from heart failure, or some other sort of internal failure, because their systems were totally exhausted.

The same goes for the human body. Even if there is a wonder drug that could push your body to work at its maximum physical potential, there are limits to consider.

Besides, in the shadow of "Crazy Horse", fear rides high among many Thai workers. Despite all the investigation, no valid answers has been found to the mystery.

For the Thai workers, some of whom are afraid that they might be next, not many options are open. Some have resorted to seeking the blessings of monks who sprinkle holy water over them and recite prayers as a means of protection against whatever threatening forces surround them. Others paint their nails red or wear women's clothing before going to bed, in order to fool the female ghosts that they believe are responsible. Some even hang red-tipped phalluses outside their houses to ward off the evil spirits blamed for the deaths.

No one could blame the workers for being superstitious about the matter, especially since they are protecting their lives. They would, in fact, do anything to give themselves that psychological sense of security – whether or not it works.

39 *Lure of the Devil's Door*

When members of a particular group of healthy people suddenly start dying in large numbers, it is certain that medical experts will be busy trying to find the cause.

It was suggested that the mysterious deaths of Thai workers in many parts of the world was caused by the use of PVC utensils in cooking their rice. The reaction produced during cooking would result in toxins that killed the workers, these claims suggested. After some consideration, however, it was found that this theory did not hold any truth. As a result, it was put aside.

Others suggested that overwork and stress could have combined to cause the deaths, leaving the symptoms of fatal heart attacks.

But if the Thai workers did suffer from it, then why not other migrant workers? After all, they are just as human as their Thai counterparts.

I believe the medical examiners and other experts studying the problem came quite close to the truth, but did not manage to pinpoint the exact cause. Science and *feng shui* are but two sides of the same coin. Just as science has its own point of view and approach to solving problems, so too does *feng shui*.

We could say that many of our characteristic traits are inherited from our parents. For example, we say that a man may have his father's temper, or his mother's patience. Sometimes a little is "handed down" from both parents. This is also true of physical features.

When an important document is reproduced on a photostat machine, its contents will be clearly visible, but the original

102

would still be the only one with a valid signature. So when we see a child who has similar features to either or both parents, we joke that he must have been made in the same factory. What I am trying to say is that many of the young Thai workers who died in their sleep could have inherited a deadly gene.

Recently, scientists in Chicago found evidence that a specific gene may be the cause of alcoholism in some individuals. They warned that not everyone with the gene was doomed to be an alcoholic, because further research showed that more than one gene was involved.

Scientists at the University of Texas Health Science Centre in San Antonio and the University of California in Los Angeles said they had studied the brain tissue of 35 alcoholics and 35 non-alcoholics after death. The study found there was a strong connection between alcoholism and genes. Among the group of alcoholics, the gene was present in 77 per cent of the cases; for the non-alcoholics, 72 per cent did not have that gene. More studies are being done for the benefit of 28 million American children of alcoholics, who may be at risk themselves.

To get rid of lallang, you must remove its roots – trimming it will only encourage the weed to grow faster. The same applies when you are faced with a serious problem. You must seek its true source, or you will be merely barking up the wrong tree.

To analyse the Thai syndrome, you must know some of the history. At one time, colonial "masters" held sway in many parts of Asia. In Malaya, Borneo, Burma and India, the British ruled. The Dutch controlled Indonesia and the East Indies, while the Spanish had the Philippines and the French, Indochina.

China itself came under the rule of the Khans of Mongolia, while in the late eighteenth century, many foreign powers carved a slice of the country for themselves. These powers, like the British, French, Russians, Americans, Germans and Japanese, forced six new Treaty Ports to be opened after the signing of the Treaty of Tientsin. Later, in December 1941, the Japanese war machine steam-rolled over most of Asia.

Whether due to diplomacy, military strength or what-have-you, history shows that Thailand has never been colonized or conquered. As the people were never dominated by any foreign power, they called themselves Thais, or "Free People".

In the belief of *feng shui,* the "Free People" can only enjoy true freedom within the boundaries of their own country. Since they were never dominated by other forces before, it is believed that once they leave their country to work for others, they fall under the shadow of this mysterious syndrome.

It is different with those who leave frequently for business trips, perhaps, or who serve their country on foreign soil.

Another point to note is that nearly all the 15 workers who died in Singapore this year are from north-eastern Thailand. The north-east is known as the "devil's door" in *feng shui,* so it could be easier for the soul snatcher to claim the lives of those who reside in this direction.

As I see it, a solution through *feng shui* would be to carry a locket containing soil from his country. This way, no matter where he goes, the worker would still be in contact with his homeland at all times.

40 *Isle of the Upturned Tortoise*

The island of Penang is well-known for its slow-paced lifestyle where the inhabitants go about life in a leisurely, unhurried pace. That quality has endeared it to tourists seeking peace and quiet, and especially pensioners looking for a place to spend the rest of their days in relaxation. Just like a tortoise, you might think. And you won't be wrong. From the air, the island looks like a tortoise on its back. This has its good and bad points.

To the Chinese, the tortoise symbolizes good health and longevity. Good health precedes others because with health one can seek wealth. As such, the tortoise is also associated with riches. But if this is true, Penang has not completely lived up to these expectations.

The British established their first settlement in Malaya on the island in 1786 when Captain Francis Light raised the Union Jack. Historians have conflicting views on the reason for the founding of Penang. Some say it is because of the island's strategic position which served the navy well. But modern research has tended to indicate that the motive was purely commercial as Britain's major need in the eighteenth century was for a new port of call on the route to the Far East, particularly to China.

But Penang failed to meet the expectations of the East India Company which led Sir Stamford Raffles to look for an alternative base. This resulted in the founding of Singapore to the south twenty-three years later.

No matter how one looks at it, Penang still resembles an upturned tortoise with its legs hanging in mid-air, struggling to get back on solid ground. This is one of the reasons it has lagged behind Singapore in terms of commerce and development.

Let's look at the island itself. Its heart is located on the right side where there is much activity. And the spot is precisely where the foothill settlement of Air Itam is located, site of the famous Kek Lok Si Pagoda. The stretch with the next best *feng shui* starts from the hamlet of Pulau Tikus in the north-east, along the coast of Fort Cornwallis in the Esplanade which faces the north channel. Then comes the head of the tortoise: from Tanjung Bungah to the beach resort of Batu Ferringhi. This is now a thriving tourist belt.

To *feng shui* masters, Penang is known simply as the "Island of the Upturned Tortoise". One can confidently say that it is suited for pensioners and for those who like a life of leisure – like a tortoise sunbathing on its back?

106

41 *The Wall that Unites a Country*

In November 10, 1989, the world saw the crumbling of one of man's most infamous structures – the Berlin Wall. Built in 1961 by the East Germans to stop its citizens from fleeing to the free world, it divided friends and families. Eighty people were killed while trying to scale the wall. Its demolition marked the final meltdown of the cold war which had for years divided the East and West.

Walls figure prominently in *feng shui*. Many build walls around their properties or homes to protect their belongings from intruders and thieves. Walls also serve as a physical reminder of the scope and area of a person's property – what lies within the wall is his and what is beyond is none of his business.

Some have even gone to the extent of hiring guards, placing barbed wire and installing sophisticated electronic surveillance equipment to ensure their safety and keep out intruders.

Building a wall in the middle of one's compound could also mean separating a large family into feuding camps. This often happens when a wealthy patriarch passes away without leaving a will and there is a dispute over the property.

The situation may prompt the man's kin to divide or wall up the contested property into what they believe is their share.

But not all walls have a negative effect.

One famous example is the Great Wall of China. Many scholars of ancient Chinese history believe that the structure was built solely as a protective perimeter against invaders. The blood thirsty Tartars and marauding Mongolians from the north, who often plundered Chinese villages, were forces to be reckoned with. But the real reason for the Wall's construction is still debatable.

China in those days was divided into at least 100 different states ruled by warlords, feudal lords and warriors rewarded for their loyalty. Civil wars were common and the future uncertain and full of danger.

Boundaries between states were like a moving line of sand which shifted with each battle. Four states stood out among the warring factions – Ch'in, Chin, Chi and Chu.

In 246BC, a boy of four, King Wen, ascended the Dragon Throne and founded the Ch'in Dynasty. Later he adopted the title Ch'in Shih Huang Ti – the first emperor of China. During his reign, terror spread throughout the land as he mercilessly and systematically united all the states. He became the supreme leader. Those who opposed him were crushed. He is remembered for two things – the destruction of books and writings he considered subversive and the building of the Great Wall of China.

Construction of the 6,000 km Wall took ten years and resulted in the loss of many lives. Along the wall, which stretches from Shanhaiguan Pass in the east to Jiayuguan Pass in Hubei province, are 13-metre high watch towers, numbering

25,000 in all. The Wall is the only man-made structure visible from the Moon.

Looking at the map of continental Europe and China, one can see the similarity in size. Thus lies one of the best kept secrets of *feng shui*. Europe consists of many different countries, each with its own culture, language, lifestyle and system of government. It resembles a jigsaw. China, on the other hand, is united in one common language although it has as many provinces as Europe has countries. Each area, however, has its distinct dialect and clan. If there had not been a wall built, there may be many separate countries instead of just China. Chinese dialects will then become different languages instead.

And for that, the Chinese have Shih Huang Ti to thank for with a master stroke he commanded the building of the Wall and thus united the diverse country.

42 *The Path-Finder*

Getting one's bearings is important in life, in travels, even in geomancy. We will begin with a look at the compass, its beginnings and development through the ages.

It is easy to find your way around an urban setting; the numerous signposts point you in the right direction. Imagine, however, that you are trekking through dense jungle, surrounded by trees that reach high into the sky and cast all kinds of unnerving shadows in your path. The inexperienced hiker who dares enter a jungle and then lose his bearings will certainly have a harrowing time. The sounds, heat and sights of his surroundings will get to him soon, if he is not fit enough to survive.

Ask anyone experienced in trekking, exploration or wilderness survival, and he will probably tell you that one of the most important instruments to have along on such trips is the magnetic compass – a path-finder back to civilization or safety.

The Chinese compass needle always point to the South while the Western compass points to the North.

In ancient times, there was a saying which warned would-be adventurers to "travel only as far as your eyes can see, or the deep-sea devils will take your life". In those days, people believed that the entire world was but a flat piece of land surrounded by water. To go beyond the horizon – what your eyes could not see – was to sail into danger. Sea routes were largely unknown to many people and many nations, except to countries like Portugal, Spain, Holland and England.

Many brave men who sailed off to map the uncharted seas did not return. Nonetheless, the tales that circulated about "lands of plenty" lying out there spurred many to set sail.

By the thirteenth and fourteenth centuries, the race was truly on to find new sea routes and new lands. Then, in the year 1403, Admiral Ying Ching reached Malacca; his landing there brought great honour and prestige to China. The compass, which by then was being used widely in *feng shui* was brought by the ships to these lands.

The Compass

A lodestone, or a piece of iron touched by a lodestone, will align itself automatically to a magnetic North and South position. This discovery must have caused many heads to turn, but its application to navigation has been attributed to various origins, from the Chinese to the Greeks, the Etruscans to the Finns – these and other races have claimed credit as originators of the compass.

In the ninth century, the Chinese were trading in the Persian Gulf. There was no evidence that the compass was used. The earliest report of the use of the compass was in a work entitled *P'ing Chou K'o Ta'u,* and the date given was at the end of the eleventh century.

When the Europeans first made it through the Eastern seas, it was noticed that the compass used by the Chinese was different from theirs. Therefore, it was suggested that the compass must have been invented independently in Europe and in China.

The invention of the compass has also been claimed by the Arabs who were at the time superior in scientific learning and early navigation skills.

The earliest reference to the use of a compass has been traced to Mohammed at Awfi; it is mentioned in a collection of Persian anecdotes written in 1232. An Arabian writer named Bailak Kibdjaki shows in his *Merchant's Treasure* (1282) that the floating compass, a magnetized needle floating in water by means of a piece of wood or a reel, was used in that instance.

In the early twelfth century, sea captains who navigated the Indian seas used a sort of fish made out of hollow iron. When it was thrown into the water, its head would point north.

The earliest authenticated use of compasses were in China, 1100AD; Arabia, 1200AD; and Scandinavia, 1250AD. The earliest record of the compass being used in western Europe was in 1187. Is there a compass that pre-dates all these?

Olden Days' Travels: An ancient Sinan-Chinese Compass.

43 *Legend of the Compass*

The earliest documented and authenticated use of the compass is said to have been in the eleventh century AD. If the legend

about Emperor Shih Huang Ti is to be believed, then the compass was first used 1,300 years earlier!

One thing about history is that the longer it exists, the more distortions occur. Therefore the number of legends and myths that often grow around actual events. It takes an open, disciplined mind to see beyond these stretched truths to look at what really happened.

It is like finding the magnificently-carved pommel of an ancient sword embedded in rock. You would be left wondering what lies beyond, and come up with all sorts of theories as to what the sword looks like, if you did not have the patience to chip away the rock slowly until the sword stood revealed.

The legend we intend to look beyond is that surrounding the compass. According to popular belief, the Emperor Shih Huang Ti fought an epic battle against the rebellious prince Ch'ih Yu during the Chin Dynasty, from 221-207BC. The prince's sorcerers conjured up a mystic mist to screen the movement of his troop, leaving the imperial forces blindly plodding about in search of the enemy.

Chaos reigned during those frightening moments, when the army crashed into itself – and it seemed that the prince would be victorious, until the emperor played his trump card.

It was a chariot on which was mounted a human figure whose outstretched arm always pointed south. It so happened that the prince's army had taken up position in the south, so the chariot led the way to the enemy – and victory.

The rebels were rounded up and their leaders executed. There could have been a "magnetic chariot" in use that day, although any proof of its existence has been lost with the passage of time.

The earliest documented and authenticated use of the compass is therefore said to have been in the eleventh century AD. If the legend about Emperor Shih Huang Ti is to be believed, then the compass was first used 1,300 years earlier.

A myth is no longer a myth when concrete evidence catches up with it. This proved true of a recent finding in China, when a few hundred very old compasses were excavated. These ancient compasses proved to be very different.

A compass normally comes in a single unit with the needle fixed to run freely from the centre to its magnetic direction. The ancient compass that was found, also known as the Sinan compass, comes in two separate units. One of them is a square flat metal plate measuring 7 cm x 7 cm. In the centre of the square is a circle with a diameter of 3.3 cm. On the metal square, you can also see the eight direction of the *Pakua I-Ching* signs. The other unit is a metal spoon with a length of 3.8 cm. When the spoon is left in the centre of the compass, thus joining them into a single unit, the action takes place. As the spoon has a magnetic propensity, it will spin with its own accordance before finally coming to a halt. Note that the spoon handle points north while the concave area points south.

44 *The Secret of the Spoon Compass*

Earlier we talked about the origins of the compass and its usage, and now our discussion ends with the Spoon compass – which is said to be the oldest in the world.

To analyse this compass (known as the Sinan compass), we must take into consideration its age and usage. According to the commonly held belief, the Sinan compass was used during the Western Han Dynasty (206BC-AD24). Most likely, it was invented by a secret sect of Taoists because you can easily recognize the Taoist symbol of the *Pakua I-Ching* signs on the flat metal plate component of the compass. There are eight directions on the plate, symbolizing the eight pillars of Taoism on which their philosophy is based. In the centre of the square metal plate, a circle dominates – wherein lies the invisible symbol of the *yin* and the *yang,* the two forces of Nature. The creator of the compass also knew that the world was circular in shape, unlike the many who believed otherwise during those times.

The other unit, which is the magnetic spoon, acts as a direction-finder. Here we have another example of the forces of *yin* and *yang* at play. When it is placed on the plate, and aligns itself according to the pull of the magnetic forces, a few things may be noted about its alignment.

First, the highest point of the spoon points northward. Geographically, northern China has high, hostile mountains which in those days were the dwelling-place of marauding bar-

116

barians. In addition to all this, the harsh, cold climate and inhospitable terrain made the north an undesirable place to live.

In the south, however, the climate is warm and soothing, and the soil just right for growing crops. It is also where the ocean lies, and where merchants and traders carry out much of their trade. Because of these factors, the south was considered a better place to live. Because of this belief, the Chinese have always oriented their compass needles to point to the south. In-

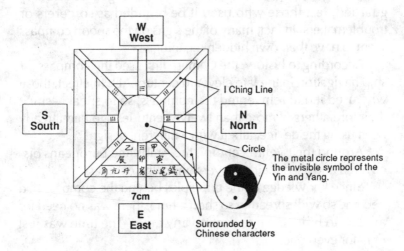

The metal circle represents the invisible symbol of the Yin and Yang.

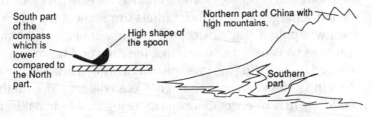

The magnetic spoon which points to the North represents the geographical landscape of China. As the northern part of China is high, so is the spoon. The south part is the lower land also shown similarly by the spoon.

South part of the compass which is lower compared to the North part.

High shape of the spoon

Northern part of China with high mountains.

Southern part

deed, the tip of the "handle" of the spoon compass points to the south.

Why was there such a huge gap of 1,300 years between the estimated time of origin of the Sinan compass, and the earliest recorded use of the compass in China (previously held to have been in the eleventh century AD). One of the theory is that certain groups of people believed that their ideas and practices were too far ahead of the times, and so confined knowledge of these things to their own circles. This knowledge was carefully guarded, lest those who used it be branded as sorcerers or troublemakers. In fact, many of the signs on the spoon compass seem to have their own hidden meaning.

According to history, the Chinese first used the compass for ship navigation in the late eleventh century AD. In effect, those who used it had reinvented the compass, so to speak – since their forefathers of more than twelve centuries ago had already been using the device, albeit with a different design!

Around the twelfth century, the Arabs and Europeans discovered and used their own versions of the compass.

Since knowledge of the principles behind the compass had become so widespread in so short a time, there was no need for anyone to hide that information any more. The time was just right for everyone.

Many developments and discoveries have been swept "under the rug" in the past. For example, in the mid eighteenth century, a French engineer by the name of Du Perron presented the young King Louis XVI with a "military organ". This instrument discharged twenty-four bullets simultaneously when a lever was pulled. The device, the forerunner of the machine-gun, was considered so lethal that the King and his ministers rejected it – branding the inventor an enemy of humanity.

Who knows? As archaeologists keep digging around the world, we may discover more and more instances when the ancients really knew much more than they allowed historians to record.

45 *That Which the Naked Eye Cannot See*

We should not presume that what we cannot see does not exist. It is usually the deeds of our conscious minds that make fools of us all, in failing to realize that some happenings in the physical world can be related to the unforeseen forces which surround us.

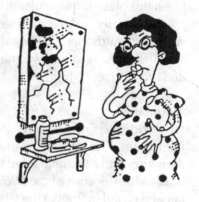

Before China opened its doors to the rest of the world, it was seen as a land of myth and mystery. "Secrets" like kungfu, the balancing of *yin* and *yang* in maintaining health and the science of acupuncture drew large crowds of westerners to China to seek knowledge of these mysteries.

Of the many who came, one particular group of professionals comprising doctors, dietitians, biologists, chemists and geologists bundled themselves into jeeps and embarked on a low-profile expedition. Their journey took them into uncharted territory, over unfamiliar mountains and across inhospitable deserts, before they finally came to a village where an unusually high number of twins had been born.

After a day of much-needed rest, the team set about its business. The doctors lined up the villagers to examine them; the

119

chemists tested the wells and river water; the geologists examined the mineral contents of the soil; and the dietitians just queried the villagers on their eating habits.

After two weeks, the team members met to discuss what they had discovered. Each member came forth to disclose his findings, and the group realized there was nothing special about the water, soil, diet, or even the people.

The leader, Kent McDonald, told the rest of them to pack up for the return trip. While everyone went about the business of pulling stakes, McDonald stood atop a high vantage point outside the village contemplating the forces of nature that had given this place its particular distinction.

Eventually, he decided to join his colleagues but as he walked towards them, he heard a shrill voice from behind him. Turning, he saw an old woman gesturing wildly towards him and trying to reach him.

Mountains
He decided to find out what she wanted and was joined by his interpreter. The interpreter spoke to the old woman at length, then turned to McDonald and told him the villagers frequently bore twins because of the two identical mountains that stood tall and proud in front of the village.

Whether or not McDonald believed this, he at least had an unusual tale to relate to his family and colleagues when he got home.

When the ancient Greeks were at the peak of their civilization they too had their own beliefs which closely matched those of the Chinese, especially when it comes to child-bearing.

Bedrooms and other main rooms in a house often had paintings and busts of handsome Greek gods and beautiful goddesses at strategic point. By decorating their homes in this way, the Greeks believed that during a woman's pregnancy, the expectant mother would somehow subconsciously "programme" the looks of the gods and goddesses into her unborn offspring.

When the baby was born, it would have the profile of a handsome Greek god or, if a girl, the beauty of a goddess. How much truth there is in these ancient ways, we certainly do not know.

Among the Chinese, there are also many beliefs surrounding pregnancy. One of them calls for a "ban" on any renovation work in a house where a pregnant woman lives. It is held that the noise and dust will cause the expectant mother much discomfort and consequently, her irritation will have a negative effect on the baby's appearance. Mirrors and glasses are also treated carefully so that they do not shatter and cause scarring of any sort on the child's face.

Whether or not these things are to be believed is not the point; to most Chinese, they would just as soon not take the risk that it might be true after all. Similarly, we should not scoff at things that are said of unseen forces and elements simply because we cannot detect them with our own limited senses.

46 *Render unto Caesar*

Feng shui is an art which is complicated even to the practising professional. Since there is no short cut to the acquiring of this talent, some schools of thought hold that it normally takes two years for a person just to build a foundation on these studies. It takes many more years of dedicated study after that, under the watchful eye of a master, before one is ready to set out on this kind of profession.

In ancient times, a talent for environmental balancing was cultivated to a very high degree by practising Taoists, ascetic monks and philosophers who had an understanding of Nature's secrets. Living in secluded monasteries and caves perched high up on rugged mountains, these practitioners found the solitude and atmosphere they needed to meditate and relax. On top of all that, the imperial government in China at the time also played an important role in acting as the guardians or keepers of these institutions, so they could flourish.

Land reforms and special financial allowances were allotted. With the novices looking after the farms, the abbot and some chosen disciples would occasionally leave the mountains to buy essential goods which they could not produce themselves. Because most of their material needs were taken care of by the state, many of these people had no worries about shelter and food. All they had to do was follow the rigid rules and regulations of whatever sect they had chosen to follow in life.

If a scholar and monk also happened to be adept in the art of *feng shui,* he would be much sought after by all. But because of the vows he had taken to achieve such levels of training in

122

the first place – and the vow of poverty was often one of them – he could not demand any fee as the host's hospitality was deemed payment enough.

In fact, most of the time the scholar monk would end up getting a red packet with an undisclosed amount inside insisted upon by the host as a token of appreciation and a "return" of good luck for his services. Businessmen who had made it big after their consultation would even contribute funds for a good cause – raising more temples and monasteries.

WHAT? YOU NOW CHARGE FOR THE SERVICE. I THOUGHT IT'S FREE.

GEOMANCER

But affairs of state are never the same forever. When times of crisis and war came, the temples and monasteries were no longer a safe place. Soon, they were abandoned. When this happened, the deposed king went into hiding. The winds of change had blown a new course for the institutions that had once depended upon the government for protection, leaving them to fend for themselves.

Adaptation is the word – where new rules had to be followed in order to survive. The practising geomancer or scholar then had to adjust to a new world, styled by a different approach to this rule. Materialism reigned and suddenly, everything had its price. The geomancer soon learned that he had no choice but to charge a fee for his services because the state no longer supported him. Most of the clients understood and paid their dues. But some of them seemed to think the geomancer could survive on spiritual reward alone and so did not pay him.

Geomancy is not an easy profession, especially when there are clients who seem to be around solely to give geomancers a tough time. For instance, there was a rich young man who invited a geomancer to his residence to help plan his new house according to the rules of *feng shui.*

Studying the site of the proposed area, he returned to the client's house for further discussion. By then, the client had "armed" himself with an architect who had also brought along the blueprints for the house.

There followed an open discussion among the geomancer, the architect and the client. Because of the geomancer's vast experience, the discussion was over within an hour, leaving the rest of the work to be completed by the architect.

Two months went by without any news from the client, so the geomancer decided to submit a bill for the job. The very next day, he received a rude call from the client, who was screaming his head off on the other end of the line. The client was angered by the fact that the geomancer had charged him a fee. The geomancer managed to tell the disgruntled client that he could have his services "on the house".

Embarrassed, the client agreed to pay a reduced amount in the form of a red packet, the amount being calculated on the basis of the time spent on the job.

When the geomancer was later asked by a close friend what he thought of it, he just chuckled and said that if all his clients paid him by the hour, he would take much longer to do his job!

Learning to waste time on a *feng shui* project in order to earn a better income can be profitable business for a geomancer. Some advice for first-timers consulting geomancers: be diplomatic, check on the amount or estimate for a particular job. Otherwise, it would definitely lead to embarrassment.

Index